STO

A   Y0-BYU-032

DISCARDED

12-14-72

Westward by Canal

Westward
by
Canal

by Ruth Franchere

THE MACMILLAN COMPANY, NEW YORK, NEW YORK

COLLIER-MACMILLAN LIMITED, LONDON

Copyright © 1972 Ruth Franchere. All rights reserved. No part of this book may be reproduced or transmitted in any form or by any means, electronic or mechanical, including photocopying, recording or by any information storage and retrieval system, without permission in writing from the Publisher.

The Macmillan Company
866 Third Avenue, New York, N.Y. 10022
Collier-Macmillan Canada Ltd., Toronto, Ontario

Library of Congress catalog card number: 71–185217
Printed in the United States of America

10   9   8   7   6   5   4   3   2   1

Map by Rafael Palacios

Picture Credits: Page 66—Brown Brothers; pages 104, 105, 106—Carnegie Library of Pittsburgh; page 107 (top)—Cincinnati Historical Society; pages 62 (top), 63 (top), 64, 103, 107 (bottom)—Culver Pictures, Inc.; pages 61, 65, 108—Historical Pictures Service—Chicago; page 63 (bottom)—Radio Times Hulton Picture Library.

To Michael Hoyt Hinds

1722900

ODESSEY

Contents

*Illustrations appear between pages 61 and
66 and pages 103 and 108.*

MAJOR CANAL ROUTES

CANADA

ST. LAWRENCE R.

RICHELIEU R.

LAKE CHAMPLAIN

VERMONT

NEW HAMPSHIRE

NEW YORK

LAKE ONTARIO

OSWEGO R.

Rome

MOHAWK R.

CHAMPLAIN CANAL

Lockport   ERIE   CANAL

Rochester   SENECA R.   Syracuse   Utica   Schenectady   Troy

Buffalo   Albany

HUDSON R.

MASSACHUSETTS

LAKE ERIE

CONNECTICUT

Cleveland

PENNSYLVANIA

SUSQUEHANNA R.

DELAWARE R.

PENNSYLVANIA & OHIO CANAL

Akron

(GRAND CANAL)
PENNSYLVANIA CANAL

JUNIATA R.

SCHUYLKILL R.

NEW JERSEY

Harrisburg

Pittsburgh   Johnstown   Hollidaysburg

Philadelphia

Wheeling

Columbia

OHIO R.

MARYLAND

DELAWARE BAY

WEST VIRGINIA

D.C.

DELAWARE

POTOMAC R.

CHESAPEAKE BAY

ATLANTIC OCEAN

VIRGINIA

APPALACHIAN MOUNTAINS

NORTH CAROLINA

1

A Way West

Long before the Revolutionary War, American colonists knew that a great barrier, the Appalachian Mountains, split their country into two parts. According to early explorers, the long chain of mountains stretched like an ancient wall from the Canadian border to what later became Alabama.

Colonial leaders worried. They feared that unless a way was found to break through the barrier and allow people to move freely across the mountains, some other nation might lay claim to the valuable land on the other side.

No one was more deeply aware of this problem than George Washington. When he was only sixteen years old, he had worked as a surveyor's helper, traveling many miles through the Allegheny Mountains, a part of

the Appalachian chain. He helped to survey a route up
the Potomac River and a trail over the mountains Soon
he was convinced that a road must be built across the
barrier, wide and safe enough to transport families and
produce back and forth in big, heavy wagons.

Washington talked to everyone he knew about his
idea. He wrote many letters and even published articles
in newspapers. But he was still too young to have much
influence.

When he was older, he made other long trips westward through the mountains and was surprised each
time to see how many men had somehow got their
families to the rich Ohio valleys on the other side.

But how poor and despondent they were. They had
been encouraged by land speculators to push through
the wilderness trails taking only their families, a few
bundles of clothes, a horse or two, and some cattle and
sheep. They could grow tremendous crops in Ohio,
they were told, and swift rivers would quickly carry
their produce to markets.

But now they knew better. The swift rivers were full
of obstructions—rapids and falls, rocks and sand bars,
islands of dead trees and driftwood. In late summer,
when corn and wheat were ready for market, most of
the rivers became too shallow to float a loaded raft.
Besides, where were the markets?

The Ohio River, although it required many portages,
could carry a raft or flat barge to the Mississippi River.
From there, with luck, a man could float his produce
down to New Orleans, which belonged to Spain.

But all the other early settlers had to use the same market. In peak season it was so glutted with men trying to sell their corn, wheat, and salted pork that prices dropped. Few were able to get enough money for their produce to pay for transporting it. Unable to buy the staples that their families needed, settlers broke up their rafts and barges, exchanged the wood for a sackful of goods, and angrily trudged all the way home.

That was the situation west of the Alleghenies.

Not long before the Revolutionary War, a good many other men were dreaming up plans to solve this same problem of providing a route between East and West. "Internal Improvements" became their slogan.

One persistent idea was to dig a passageway—a canal—from Delaware Bay to Chesapeake Bay. From that point there was a possible route up the Susquehanna River and over the mountains to the head of the Ohio River. The rivers would have to be cleared of most of the obstructions and in some places portages would have to be provided. A road would have to be cut through the mountains between the two rivers. But to some it seemed like a possible solution.

A group of Philadelphia businessmen even paid two hundred dollars to have a canal survey made. In time, however, they decided that this route was too far south of Philadelphia to be of much use to them, and so they abandoned the project.

William Penn had another idea. The Schuylkill River ran directly to Philadelphia. Some distance upriver a branch of the Schuylkill reached out toward a branch of the Susquehanna. A canal could easily connect them and provide a much better route for Philadelphians, he believed.

The Revolutionary War soon occupied the thoughts of everyone, especially General Washington, and for a time plans for any routes were dropped. But later this last one was revived and a company was chartered to build the canal.

George Washington, then president, went out to inspect the work. He found a few locks which "appeared admirably constructed." But as soon as the company got into difficult construction work, it ran out of money and gave up.

Other ideas were brought forth. Companies were organized and stock was sold. But only a few very short canals, from one to three miles long, were completed. These were usually around falls and rapids and did make river travel somewhat easier.

Meanwhile, Easterners were clamoring for a way west. Enthusiastic letters had drifted back from the pioneers beyond the mountains. Articles in newspapers described in flowery language that glorious place where no poverty existed, where even the poorest settlers could become landowners and have lives of ease and comfort.

Although most of these reports greatly exaggerated the paradise that awaited all comers, they correctly described the amazingly deep, rich black loam in what they called The West—which meant any place from the Appalachians to beyond the Mississippi River in

Spanish territory. They failed to mention, however, the settler's heartbreaking labor of chopping down the giant trees and of planting corn among the stumps until he could dig them out, one by one, or burn them out. And especially they did not mention the terrible loneliness of the wives and children, whose nearest neighbors might be many miles away through the black forests.

But people believed the reports, passed letters from one family to another, wore out newspaper accounts, and dreamed of paradise. A Connecticut farmer wearily clearing stones from the clay soil of his hilly farm had reason to wonder why he too should not go west to where he could easily grow one hundred bushels of wheat to the acre.

And the factory worker earning his meager wages for long days of labor hoarded his pennies while he dreamed of having some of that land that he could buy for only $1.25 an acre.

Every day, immigrants landing on the docks at eastern cities clutched their belongings—homemade wooden plows, a few household utensils, bundles of worn clothes—and turned longing eyes westward. For even in Europe, stories about the land behind the mountains of America made daily news.

Only one thing stood in the way of massive migration —that great stone wall, the Appalachian mountain range. Few of the dreamers were willing to leave most of their possessions behind and set off on foot along the old Indian trails. They waited, but impatiently.

In 1796, Congress made a very small gesture. It agreed to allow a man named Ebenezer Zane to cut a trail at an angle through the wilderness of public land in Ohio Territory. The trail was only wide enough for a man on a horse, perhaps leading a packhorse and a few other animals. Although this was one way of helping the travelers who were already on the other side of the mountains to avoid the treacherous and unpredictable rivers, it did not help the Easterners get across the mountains. The route, known as Zane's Trace, became somewhat wider with use, but it was never really suitable for wagon travel.

Meanwhile patchworks of toll roads, called turnpikes, were being laid out along important trade routes. Sometimes farmers or groups of neighbors with adjoining land would clear a wagon track through their properties. Soon companies were chartered by the dozens to build roads across government land. They sold stock to raise money for clearing and fencing.

As soon as a road was finished, a gate was placed at each end to stop wagons or riders from going through. On busy roads, someone was stationed nearby to collect the tolls and open the gate. On lesser roads, a rope was attached to a bell which would summon the farmer or his wife.

Tolls varied, depending upon the size of the load, the number of people and animals going through, and the honesty or temperament of the gatekeeper. But toll roads were too expensive for the average Easterner who was saving his money to buy western land. And the cost of moving freight by these turnpikes was staggering.

In 1802, the federal government passed an "enabling act" which promised that 5 per cent of the money from the sale of government land in Ohio would be used for roads. These were to reach from navigable eastern rivers across the mountains to the Ohio River and on through the new state of Ohio.

Demands for the government to start building such roads came from the East and the West. In that same year a royal order from Spain had closed New Orleans to American trade, and the settlers were desperate for a market. But four years went by before Congress passed a law for laying out a road four rods (sixty-six feet) wide from the Potomac to Ohio by the shortest route.

The shortest route, it was determined, was the very one that George Washington had wanted many years before. But this road was to reach farther down the Ohio River—to Wheeling, Ohio—where it could join Zane's Trace. From the head of the Potomac to Wheeling was about ninety miles.

More years passed while the clamor grew louder. Not until 1811 was construction started.

The new road was finally opened to Wheeling in 1817, although it was not entirely completed. It was named the Cumberland Road, but most people called it the National Road, for it was the first road financed by the national government. In 1818, the first mail coaches ran between Washington and Wheeling.

On a map, the road looked fine. But through the mountains it looked quite different. It was a rocky, makeshift road—improperly drained and buttressed. Before it was finished, the first part was beginning to crumble. In 1822, Congress had to pass another bill "for the preservation and repair of the Cumberland Road."

In spite of its poor condition, people in the middle Atlantic states, especially the upland farmers of Virginia, hailed the road as the first great breakthrough to the West. At once a steady stream of traffic began to move across it.

Huge Conestoga wagons loaded with freight gouged deep ruts in the thin surface of rock. Farm wagons loaded to overflowing bumped and jogged over the crumbling surface. While the farmers walked beside their wagon teams trying to avoid the largest chuckholes, their wives and children trudged up the mountain herding the cattle, sheep, hogs, and even chickens. At the sharp warning from a stagecoach horn they scrambled to the soft shoulder of the road, calling frantically to the terrified animals as the swaying stage dashed by. Mail coaches too covered the distance at a reckless pace, endangering the lives and property of the slow movers.

Many an animal was killed or lost on the Cumberland Road. And many an axle was cracked or a wheel broken.

But the steady stream of movers using every sort of conveyance, even high-wheeled carriages and two-wheeled carts, went on. They were bent on getting a parcel of land for themselves in the West, although few had any idea where it might be.

When at last they arrived at Wheeling and rode a ferry across the Ohio River, they found that Zane's

Trace was much worse than the Cumberland Road. Logs lay where they had fallen. Stumps still cluttered the way. Underbrush grew back where nature had intended it to be. Yet many movers took the Trace, preferring to face hardship on land rather than to risk danger on the Ohio River.

The Cumberland Road did open a difficult way west for people living in the middle states, but it was much too far away for New Englanders and New Yorkers. Their problem was as acute as ever.

2

Canal to Lake Erie

Indians had a route west from the northern colonies. Some of their portages were secret, but in time it became known that they entered the Mohawk River from the Hudson about 150 miles above New York City in the area of the village of Albany.

First they portaged around the Cohoes Falls—usually called the Great Falls because of the tremendous drop. Then they paddled their canoes up the Mohawk against a swift and shallow current, pulled them across sand bars, dragged or carried them around other falls and rapids, and at last reached the source of the river. On they went, taking advantage of streams and river branches until they reached the Oswego River which carried them north to Lake Ontario.

From colonial times, many men suggested that this waterway be cleared for use by the white men, for it was the only real cut in the long mountain chain.

General George Washington, always searching for a way west, traveled on horseback through upper New York State in 1783 and 1784. He too believed that the Mohawk River region might be developed for east-west traffic by water. However, he did not favor the Indian route that turned north to Lake Ontario, thus leading to British territory. No American could travel west that way through the Great Lakes, for the Niagara Falls barred the entrance to Lake Erie. The only water route west from the Mohawk would have to be dug all the way to Lake Erie.

Meanwhile, some people did use the east-west route through what was generally called "York State," but at what cost! They had no trouble getting to Albany by boat, for the Hudson was a wide, placid river on which fleets of sailing sloops carried freight and passengers between New York City and Albany. Or they could get there in any simple craft rigged with a sail.

The Mohawk was entirely different. It came boiling down from the west, and few white men could attempt to make the difficult portage. But wagoners were available at Albany, for a stiff fee, to take them to Schenectady over a rough turnpike seventeen miles long.

At Schenectady boatmen were waiting to relieve the travelers of more of their money. They loaded them and all their baggage into very shallow, flat-bottomed barges with square ends, called bateaux, and poled them up the Mohawk River, making portages where necessary.

Poling was difficult enough, even for a strong, experienced bateauman. He pushed the boat upriver against the swift current by leaning the butt of a long pole against his well-callused shoulder and thrusting the iron tip into the river bottom.

Bateaux usually had several polers who "walked" the boat upriver. Standing backward at the bow, a man thrust his pole against a rock in the river bottom. Leaning hard against it he walked to the stern while the boat moved upstream under his feet. Meanwhile another man had taken his place at the bow and had begun to walk. Large bateaux had polers on both sides. Back and forth they went all day long.

Powerful bateaumen acquainted with every whim of the river could successfully move men and baggage in this way, but it was no work for inexperienced farmers or city men.

In some places where portages were necessary, farmers hauled the bateaux on huge flat wagons pulled by oxen. This too was costly.

How far the travelers got depended upon the time of year, the condition of the river, and the amount of money they had. Some of them settled along the Mohawk, cleared away trees, and tried to make a life for themselves and their families. Others pushed farther west. But all now knew what lay between them and Albany. They could only hope that someday someone would find a means of clearing an easy route for them.

Soon after President Washington made his suggestion, an engineer named Christopher Colles, an Irishman who had been surveyor-general for the colonial governor of the province of New York, asked the legislature for permission to remove the obstructions from the Mohawk. The legislators granted him permission and in 1785 appropriated $125 for the work. For this small amount, Colles could only make a survey. But it was the first real survey of the area. He published his report and proposed that seven miles of canals be built around three waterfalls.

For the next thirty years, the subject of making an inland waterway across the state was discussed, debated, and argued. Dozens of ideas were brought forth, some of them fantastic. Many were the arguments between those who wanted merely to improve the rivers and those who wanted to build a real canal all the way across the state to Lake Erie.

In 1772, Benjamin Franklin, that great thinker who was always far ahead of his time, had written a letter from London to Mayor Rhodes of Philadelphia explaining why he preferred canals to natural waterways. He said: "Rivers are ungovernable things, especially in hilly countries; canals are quiet and very manageable. . . ." He also advised that if America should decide to build canals, an experienced canal engineer should be obtained from England, where many canals, dikes, and locks were being constructed. But America did not take his advice.

At last one man undertook a part of the work that had been suggested. With a grant of money from the state, in 1792 General Philip Schuyler formed the Western Inland Lock Navigation company. With no experience to draw on, he started the construction of a canal around Little Falls, about forty miles beyond Schenectady.

He hired three hundred men for the work. But since no one really knew how to go about constructing locks, they wasted much time standing around, arguing, and waiting to be told what to do.

By 1795, the company had completed less than a mile of canal containing five wooden locks. Later it cut a crude ditch between the upper Mohawk River and Wood Creek, thus making a way for small boats to go farther west than the Mohawk valley. But even with more money from the state of New York, the company could do no more. In time the state took it over.

Meanwhile, the little canal did help greatly in getting freight across the state. Larger boats could make the trip in much less time for only one-third the cost. Traffic increased enormously, and so did the interest in larger and better canals.

Gouverneur Morris, a former member of the Continental Congress and an important American statesman, was one of the most enthusiastic, although impractical, canal advocates. Sometimes his enthusiasm carried him to extremes.

In 1800, he wrote in a letter to a friend that ships might "sail from London through Hudson's River into Lake Erie." Three years later he was talking about drawing water from Lake Erie "in an artificial river directly across the country to the Hudson River."

His most fantastic idea came to light some years later. He wanted to build a canal on an inclined plane that started at Lake Erie and slowly dropped to the ridge near Albany.

Since no survey of the western section had been

made, he could only estimate the differences in height of the land at the eastern and western ends and of the hills and valleys between. Later it was learned that his proposed inclined plane would have been more than 350 miles long and, in at least one place, would have been 150 feet above a valley.

But he did not allow such practical matters to dampen his enthusiasm for his project. He talked so eloquently and often poetically about his pet idea that he was able to persuade others to his way of thinking.

In general the idea of a canal to Lake Erie was becoming very popular. Newspapers, still using the slogan "Internal Improvements," carried predictions of what such a canal would do for east-west trade. The writers seemed to compete with each other in compiling statistics: "It would . . . double the value of produce in the State of Ohio." "New York would become one of the most splendid commercial cities on the face of the earth."

Men reasoned that since the federal government had financed the Cumberland Road, it would surely pay for something as grand and important as a canal to Lake Erie. Two New York legislators went confidently to Washington, D.C., to discuss the matter with President Thomas Jefferson.

But the president had his own special canal project— to connect the Potomac River to the Ohio River. He was not interested in spending money on any other canal until his own project was funded.

His response was very cold. "It is a splendid project," he said, "and may be executed a century hence. . . . It is little short of madness to think of it at this day!"

New Yorkers knew then that a canal wholly within their state must be their own responsibility.

Although many state legislators favored the building of a canal, they were reluctant to back this one. The very length of it—more than 350 miles—and especially the fact that much of it would run through swamps and almost totally uninhabited and even unexplored wilderness made them wary. Besides, America had no engineers.

But there were farsighted men among the lawmakers who knew that something drastic must be done to stimulate trade within America itself. The Embargo Act, effective from 1807 to 1809, was causing great hardships. It forbade American ships to leave American shores for European ports because of British and French violence and tyranny at sea. As a result, foreign ships did not bring manufactured goods to American ports and American raw materials were rotting in warehouses because they had no markets. Many men were out of work, and farmers could not sell their produce.

Enough votes were mustered in the state legislature to force an appropriation of six hundred dollars for the first complete survey of the proposed routes. A lawyer named James Geddes, who had done a little amateur surveying, was chosen for the work.

Even though he had to use some of his own money, Geddes, with some assistants, surveyed both the route to Lake Ontario and the route directly to Lake Erie.

The report of his surveys was impressive. Although De Witt Clinton, mayor of New York City, had not previously favored the canal, he was persuaded to second a resolution appointing a commission to study the whole idea. The resolution was passed and seven men were appointed to the commission, including Clinton and Gouverneur Morris. They were given three thousand dollars for expenses.

From that day on, De Witt Clinton's interest in the canal grew steadily. He became its most important and enthusiastic champion.

In 1811, the seven members of the canal commission traveled on horseback through the wilderness to see the canal routes for themselves. At night they slept in the open or in filthy little taverns. In spite of the primitive conditions, they were pleased by what they saw.

Among other things, they were impressed by the crude salt works at Onondaga Lake near the little village of South Salina (later named Syracuse). There many salt springs bubbled out of the earth. Men filled large iron kettles with the brine, built fires under them, and boiled away the water. The salt that remained was a valuable commodity that could bring riches to the community if the excessive freight costs to the East were reduced. An earlier explorer had estimated that the salt springs were capable of producing six thousand bushels of salt each year, which was nearly enough to supply the entire country.

The commissioners agreed that the canal must run past South Salina and thus tap this great source of freight tolls that would help to pay for the canal.

But from this point, the canal must not turn north to nearby Lake Ontario, they could see. For if it did, the salt-makers could send their product by the easy route

right up to the big lake. It would be shipped out from
there through the St. Lawrence River and down the
coast, to be sold by Canada to New York. Produce from
the vast fertile lands west of Seneca Lake would go by
the same route for the benefit of British subjects.

They all agreed that the canal must go directly to
Lake Erie. Gouverneur Morris's eloquence persuaded
them to back his "inclined plane" plan, although Clinton never really liked it. The whole project, they estimated, would cost between five and six million dollars.

New York could not possibly appropriate such a sum,
so the commissioners tried to borrow money in Europe.
But by this time America was again at war with England—the War of 1812. No one in Europe would lend
them any money at all.

They tried to get help from bordering states. Pennsylvania would not consider helping to pay for a canal
that it could never use. Besides, it had several canal
projects of its own that badly needed funding. Ohio
was very sympathetic. A canal opening a route from
Lake Erie to the Atlantic would be of enormous benefit
to the state. But Ohio was not yet ten years old and had
no money to contribute.

As time passed, however, the commissioners were
becoming more sensible. The inclined plane was a fantastic idea that would never really work, they finally
agreed. They must turn to the simpler and less expensive form that had proved very successful all over Europe—a ditch with a towpath for horses and mules,
locks to carry boats up and down hills, and aqueducts
to move them across rivers and deep valleys.

But time also worked to the disadvantage of the Erie Canal project. People on the route to Lake Ontario were determined that the canal should come their way. Those in the southern part of the state objected to paying for a canal that would do them no good. And a powerful group of politicians in New York City were opposed to spending the city's tax money on the backwoods of the state. These men also believed that all government should be run by an aristocracy. They feared that if poor and ignorant people became landowners they would soon want to run the state.

Until the war was over, little could be accomplished. But De Witt Clinton, with his experience as mayor and as a former United States senator, was a master politician. He knew that the backwoods votes were just what the canal needed. After the war, when demands for trade became louder, he decided to enlist the help of those people who had never publicly voiced their opinions.

A group of prominent, farsighted men, headed by Clinton, composed a long "memorial" setting forth the great advantages of a canal from the Hudson River to Lake Erie. It would be "a bond of union between the Atlantic and the Western States." The memorial petitioned the state to authorize construction of the canal.

Copies were sent to every town and village along the proposed route. At noisy mass meetings all across York State more than one hundred thousand enthusiastic people, including many responsible citizens of New York City, added their names to the petition.

When Clinton took his memorial with its huge list of

names to the state legislature, the lawmakers could not ignore the wishes of such a great number of voters, nearly one-tenth of the entire population of the state.

Even though the New York City faction in the legislature was united against the canal, a bill was passed authorizing construction of not only the main Erie Canal but also a branch from Lake Champlain in northeastern New York down to join the Erie near Albany.

A new, smaller commission was appointed and given twenty thousand dollars for expenses. This group elected Clinton as their president.

But the problem of getting the money for construction was still a grave one. An Internal Improvements bill had been passed by Congress in Washington, and New York had been elated over the prospect of receiving its share—about ninety thousand dollars a year. But President Madison vetoed the bill.

Still the people must have their canal. They showed their determination by electing De Witt Clinton governor of the state, giving him the greatest majority of votes ever known in New York.

Citizens made gifts not only of money but also of huge blocks of land along the right of way. For day-to-day expenses, bonds were sold to raise the money until taxes and tolls from completed sections could take over the job.

At last the Erie Canal, so long awaited, was to be built.

3

Digging Clinton's Ditch

Quickly the commissioners went into action. First they sent James Geddes to take charge of the unexplored Lake Champlain section. He was to use his own judgment in building that canal, but above all he was to finish it as quickly as possible. Then they turned their entire attention to the main canal across the state.

There were no trained engineers in the country, but Americans had already proved they could do many difficult things without formal training. The problem was to find an intelligent person who was not afraid of the job.

After some discussion, the commissioners put a country lawyer named Benjamin Wright in charge of the first work on the main canal. Like Geddes, he had done a little amateur surveying, and he had worked on the

first survey of the Erie route. If he was smart enough to
be a lawyer, they decided, he ought to be able to figure
out how to build a canal.

The next job was to decide where to begin. All
agreed that the greatest possible length of canal must
be dug in the shortest possible time. Even a few miles
of navigable water would bring in tolls that could fi-
nance future digging and quiet the critics.

In the middle section of the route, one strip about
sixty-nine miles long was relatively level. It began near
the village of Utica, ran along the upper Mohawk River
for a time, and then turned to Syracuse to tie in with
the valuable salt deposits.

Between these two settlements was the village of
Rome, where the Western Inland Lock Navigation had
cut the small canal between the Mohawk River and
Wood Creek. Businesses had grown along this cut.

The commissioners decided to bypass Rome and start
the work about half a mile south. They would proceed
both east and west at the same time along this corridor
which they called "the long level." Thus for a time they
put off tackling the grave problems of how to move
boats up or down hills or across rivers and streams.

But first this important undertaking, so long in coming, must have a proper ground-breaking ceremony.
And what better day could there be for such a great
occasion than the Fourth of July?

Property owners along the old canal were very unhappy over being ignored. But the rest of the inhabit-
ants of Rome were in a frenzy of excitement. They

could scarcely believe that their little settlement out in the wilderness, built on dry land only a few feet above the swamplands, had been chosen as the starting point for a great canal.

As they rushed to prepare for the ceremony, their heads buzzed with dreams. Some envisioned the taverns they would build, where canal travelers could dine and rest and leave part of their money. Others looked at the huge trees on their plots of land and pictured them as firewood to be shipped down to the cities on the coast, where it would bring a fine price.

While they dreamed, they cleared a place near the proposed canal site, split trees to build a platform, wheeled out a cannon, and soaked torches in oil to be lighted at the proper time.

On the morning of the great day in 1817, they put on their best clothes, grabbed their spades, and hurried to the small clearing. They lighted the torches to brighten the gloom from the surrounding forest.

The president of the village, the secretary of the canal commission, and the first contractor were all assembled when word swept through the crowd that Governor De Witt Clinton himself was on his way. In a few moments he emerged from a narrow trace through the forest, sitting tall and handsome on his gray horse, and the people sent up a wild cheer.

Then the dignitaries stepped onto the platform. Each made a short speech and handed a shiny new ceremonial spade to the next man until it reached the contractor. In silence, the people watched as he moved to the edge of the platform and lifted the first spadeful of dirt.

At once, amid the boom of the cannon, the bark of guns, and the shouts of the crowd, men rushed to the spot and began digging as though they planned to finish the canal before nightfall. Women wept, children screamed, and the day was a huge success.

After this first celebration to launch the great canal, it was considered a good omen to start all canal projects on a Fourth of July.

On the morning following the celebration, crews of local workmen, under the instruction of Benjamin Wright, invaded the deep forest in both directions from Rome, marking off the canal lines. They set five rows of red markers. One row showed where the center of the canal should be. The two rows on either side, forty feet apart, marked the width for the ditch. The outer two rows, sixty feet apart, set the limits for the clearing.

To save money, the planners had decided to clear only the necessary width, thus running a narrow corridor through the dark forest. It would not be a straight corridor, for it must swerve to avoid hills and the deepest swamps, and wherever possible jog to connect existing settlements.

Borers followed, digging holes twelve feet deep so that the engineer's crew could learn what problems they faced and try to decide how to solve them.

Soon the crews, working east and west from Rome, were far apart.

Fellers and diggers were to come next. To take charge of them, contractors were hired from the villages because they could build shacks for the workers on their own property and have the means of feeding them.

But in this sparsely settled area there were not enough workmen. And in the East, men were reluctant to sign up for the exhausting work of felling giant trees and cutting a ditch four feet deep through swamps and tangles of roots thousands of years old, even for the good wages of eighty cents a day plus food and sleeping space on the floor of a contractor's shack. They preferred to wait until the canal was built and then go west to take over the cheap, rich land they had heard so much about.

However, contractors found an inexhaustible pool from which to draw workmen for the back-breaking jobs that they had to offer.

All over Europe, times were hard. Many people were without work. The situation was especially critical in Ireland. Ship captains carrying raw material from America to industrial centers of Europe soon realized that people would make excellent cargo for the return trip. Since all who wished to emigrate could provide their own food and be packed into the holds of the ships, they could be carried at a low fare.

And so they advertised for passengers, telling tall tales of the many fine jobs available in America and filling their holds for every trip. If a man or boy could not pay for his passage, a captain would gladly take him anyway and sell his services to a canal contractor for the price of his passage.

Many desperate Europeans came to America under

these conditions. Contractors were on the docks to greet them and send them on their way at once to the canal area.

West Irishmen, called bogtrotters, were in greatest demand because it was believed that they could withstand working waist-deep in the muck of the swamps all day long, especially if they were given a measure of whiskey every hour. Soon a large percentage of the laborers on the canal were Irishmen.

The Irish brought a new way of life with them. To the staid York Staters, they seemed a wild lot. They worked hard, and when Saturday night came they were ready to relax and celebrate.

They enjoyed a good rousing night of drinking that often ended in some equally rousing fights. But in the morning, when they recovered, they were all friends again. And on Monday they willingly returned to the swamps, knowing that never in Ireland could they have hoped for such fine wages.

They brought their superstitions with them, too. They saw ghosts in the bogs and would not sleep there. They saw the little people of Irish lore—pixies and leprechauns—in the shadows and whispered to each other of what they had seen.

Most important, they brought songs into the somber wilderness. While they worked they sang the songs they had heard from their childhood. Many of these were sentimental ballads and they sang them with great feeling. Gradually they added new words to the old tunes—words about their lives on the canal.

It could have been an Irishman who first told his story in a song that was sung by the bogtrotters as they worked in the swamps:

We are digging the Ditch through the mire;
Through the mud and the slime and the mire, by heck!
And the mud is our principal hire;
Up our pants, in our shirts, down our neck, by heck!
We are digging the Ditch through the gravel,
So the people and freight can travel.

From the beginning the canal was one large experiment. The accepted method of digging a ditch was for a man to thrust his spade into the earth, lift dirt into a wheelbarrow until it was full, and then cart it away to some designated spot.

But this method did not work in the wilderness, where huge tree branches interlocked overhead and the earth in which the trees grew was a mass of intertwined roots. After weeks of striving desperately with ax and spade, workers here and there on the project began to devise better methods.

They used horses and mules to pull plows and scrapers. For stubborn roots of underbrush, someone thought of adding an extra cutting blade to the plow. Soon the work went faster.

Felling a tree was a time-consuming job requiring the help of several men until a worker scrambled up a partially cut tree one day and attached an end of a cable to the top. Back on the ground again, he wound the other end of the cable around a wheel. As he turned the wheel, he wound up the cable and thus pulled down the tree without help from anyone.

To remove a huge stump with its massive, interlocked roots was a monumental job until a group of men with imagination rigged up an amazing contraption. They called it a stump puller. It was made with a stout axle twenty inches in diameter and thirty feet long. Fastened to the axle in an ingenious way were very large wheels, thick cable, and rope.

When all were assembled and the cable was fastened to a stump, a team of strong horses or oxen, aided by seven men, could pull up the stump in a few minutes and haul it away. In fact, they could dispose of thirty to forty stumps a day—a remarkable feat.

But before ice and snow ended that first year of work, Benjamin Wright knew that too many grave problems were yet unsolved. Someone must learn more about how to build locks that would carry boats down from Utica to the level of the Hudson River and up from Syracuse to Lake Erie. He must learn the best ways of crossing rivers that might be raging torrents in the spring or shallow streams in the hot summer.

A young man named Canvass White who had signed on with one of Wright's surveying crews in 1816 had shown remarkable intelligence and ability. He was chosen by Wright and De Witt Clinton to go to England to learn all he could about canal construction.

For months Canvass White walked along the towpaths of English and European canals. In fact, he covered two thousand miles of them while he inspected every aspect of canal construction, made careful drawings, asked about materials and methods, and bought new instruments with which to make measurements and tests.

Meanwhile, one of the major problems puzzling the builders was how to construct the banks of the ditch so that they would not crumble.

The original plan was designed with this problem in mind. The sides were dug at a slant so that the bottom of the channel was only twenty-eight feet wide while the top was forty feet. Then a towpath ten feet wide alongside was elevated four feet. On this path horses or mules would pack the earth as they pulled the boats along. The opposite embankment, called the berm, gave additional protection.

But for places where the earth was sandy or gravelly, the workers searched for something to use as lining. At last they found a stiff clay that they called "the blue mud of the meadows" and packed the banks with it. On some especially difficult places they added a paving of small stones, or they covered the banks with thick sod.

When Canvass White returned from Europe, the builders were puzzling over the locks that they must construct at both ends of the long level.

A lock was planned as a boxed-off area of the canal, ninety feet long and fifteen feet wide. Gates at both ends were to hold the water or let it in or out.

If a boat came from a high level it was floated into

the box, and the gate was closed behind it. Water was slowly drained out, the other gate was opened, and the boat could float out at a lower level. If it came from a low level, the process was reversed. A boat could be "locked down" or "locked up" the canal, depending upon which way it was going.

More than fifty locks would surely be needed, it was thought, to lower boats 425 feet between Utica and the Hudson River at Albany. An undetermined number would be required to carry boats westward to Montezuma and then lift them up over sheer rocks to Lake Erie.

At times the problems of planning, building, and maintaining so many locks seemed insurmountable. And yet all involved with the canal believed that somehow each problem would be faced and solved in the short time that De Witt Clinton was allowing. He had already predicted that the whole Erie Canal would be completed by 1823.

The big question in late 1818 was whether to use wood or stone for the locks. Wood could rot in a few years, but stone required cement, which had to be imported from England at great cost.

One day, near the western part of the long level, Canvass White found a different sort of stone. Following a process that he had seen in England, he burned it, crushed it into powder, and mixed it with sand. Then he pressed it into a ball and put it into a bucket of water.

The next morning he found that the ball was as hard

as a rock. He had made America's first cement, which he called "waterproof lime."

So it was decided that wherever possible the locks would be constructed of stone set in waterpoof lime. But the gates would have to be made of wood.

Before the ice came to end the 1818 season, fifteen miles of the canal from Rome to Utica were complete. In addition, ninety-four miles of the Erie's middle section were cleared of trees and underbrush, forty-eight of these were dug, and eight more were usable and awaiting inspection. A good many wooden bridges had been built across the channel at the insistence of the property owners on each side. But already some of these had been washed away by heavy rains.

When work resumed in the spring of 1819, crews pushed westward toward Montezuma, staking, clearing, and digging. As they neared the Seneca River, they moved into the muck and scum of swamps. Soon they were working waist-deep in ground so saturated with water that they could never dry out. At night they lay in their wet clothes on the damp floors of shacks. In the mornings, still wet, they returned to the swamps.

With the heat of July came black clouds of mosquitoes and gnats. They swarmed over the helpless workers day and night, tormenting them with shrill whines and agonizing stings. No amount of slapping and arm-waving would keep the ravenous insects out of ears and noses. Eyes swollen almost shut, faces fiery and festering, the men worked on, for there was no escape.

Soon fevers struck them one by one. They ached in

every part of their bodies. When they collapsed on the floors of the shacks, they shook with chills or moaned with fevers.

Before the first frosts killed the insects, hundreds of workers died. Others barely survived, sickly and subject to fevers and chills for years to come.

Although an amazing amount of work was accomplished on the canal in 1819, it was not enough to satisfy the critics—those politicians who hated or envied De Witt Clinton and the many people who were impatient to go west. The Governor had promised them the Erie Canal by 1823, but to date not one boat had scheduled a run anywhere along what they laughingly called "Clinton's Ditch." And no progress at all had been made, so far as anyone could see, in building all those locks to carry boats up from the Hudson River.

To quiet the critics, the commissioners decided to open the completed fifteen-mile section of the canal between Rome and Utica and hold another celebration. A flat-bottomed boat was built especially for the occasion and named *Chief Engineer of Rome* in honor of Benjamin Wright.

At dawn on an October morning in 1819, hundreds of men, women, and children filled the canal bridges and crowded the towpath and berm. When the feeder channels from the Mohawk River were opened and water flowed into the canal, others rushed across fields and climbed trees to see the miracle of a man-made river rolling through the land.

At Rome, De Witt Clinton, the commissioners, and

other important citizens in tall hats boarded the *Chief Engineer of Rome*. Bells rang, cannons boomed, and people shouted as a horse stepped out along the tow-path pulling the ceremonial bark through the sparkling water.

Several hours later it was greeted at Utica by another excited crowd. The next day it made the return trip to Rome while people cheered all along the way.

For a short time the critics were silenced. Then they began sniping again.

4

Triumphs and Setbacks

The miraculous corridor of sparkling water in a long, open strip of inviting sunlight was a free meeting place and playground for canalside people. They were giddy with the newness of it.

They went swimming in it. They fished from it. Groups congregated on the towpath to talk while their cattle broke down the banks to drink the water, and their chickens, geese, and ducks pecked in the mounded gravel. In the evenings young men raced their horses along the smooth, straight path.

The serious boat owners who were trying to haul cargo along this completed section were irate. They complained to the commissioners.

At last a few rules about cluttering the channel and misusing the towpath were set up. But no one paid much attention to the rules, and few fines were collected.

During the following winter, while the canal was frozen over, boat building preoccupied most of the settlers along the right of way. Some wanted only to get onto the canal, to move about, to visit their neighbors and take part in canal gossip. Others wanted to be ready to haul people or produce at the highest rate possible.

But many talked excitedly of selling their land as soon as the canal was finished and moving west to the vast prairies. There they would not have to clear away giant trees before they could grow enormous crops to ship back east. From their midpoint on the canal, they would have a good head start and would be able to select the finest acres of prairie land for their homesites. In a few years they would be wealthy, they dreamed.

Whatever the reason, cutting, planing, and hammering went on along the canal throughout the winter months. Each man had his own idea of what a canal boat should look like. He drew his own plan or just let his creation grow as his fancy indicated.

Among the more professional projects was one large passenger boat, seventy-six feet long and fourteen feet wide, called a packet. It was designed to carry a considerable number of people for a long distance and provide them with meals and a place to sleep. When water was let into a large part of the middle section late in April, 1820, the packet was taken to Syracuse and made ready for use.

A few months later, on the Fourth of July just three years after the ground-breaking ceremony at Rome, Governor Clinton staged another huge celebration, this time at Syracuse, to commemorate the opening of this large section. The big packet was displayed as a forerunner of what the citizens of New York could soon expect to enjoy. Seventy-three other boats of all shapes, sizes, and colors clogged the canal, which had no traffic rules, and added to the excitement of the day.

Governor Clinton himself was there to enjoy another triumph in the face of increasing opposition from his enemies.

One of the biggest questions at this time was how to keep a steady flow of water in the channel, which was inclined very slightly to allow water to flow in. Where the canal was close to the Mohawk River, the problem was not serious. Channels were dug between the canal and the river, a sluice gate was constructed, and a man was stationed there to keep the water at the required depth of four feet as well as to let boats through.

But away from the Mohawk the problem was more difficult. Until the canal was connected with Lake Erie, which could supply an unlimited amount of water, the planners had to depend upon nearby lakes and creeks or build reservoirs in the hills. Even these sources were not always adequate.

No one, it seemed, had accurately determined how much water would be lost when the canal came into use. Everyone knew that a lockful of water would be lost every time a boat passed through. But no one imagined what great quantities would evaporate or be absorbed by the soil or how much could leak through the wooden gates.

Thorough lining of the canal with clay was stepped

up. And methods of conserving and reusing the water in the locks were given serious study.

Meanwhile no time could be lost, for the legislature was being urged to stop the construction of the western third of the canal until the eastern part and the Lake Champlain branch were finished. Rumors flew about that certain politicians wanted the western section dropped permanently.

The commissioners were frantic. They knew not only that Lake Erie must be tapped for the much-needed water but also that the whole idea of opening up the West depended upon their reaching that lake.

They rushed thousands of workers westward to dig the channel in the shortest possible time and to construct the necessary locks between Syracuse and Rochester. They appointed a man named Nathan Roberts, a mathematics teacher who had had only a little engineering experience, to solve the terrible problem at Lockport. There the canal must rise over the stony barricade of Niagara to reach Lake Erie.

To pacify the legislature, they also began building the twenty-five locks in the eastern section between Schenectady and Utica—a rise of nearly two hundred feet in about seventy miles.

The whole strip between Schenectady and Rochester was 220 miles long, nearly two-thirds of the entire canal as it had been planned. Clinton was determined to do what everyone said was impossible—to complete all this work in three years. If he could accomplish this miracle, no one would dare to stop the canal project.

He changed his first prediction that the canal would

be completed in 1823. Because of early setbacks, he
said, the date would now be 1825.

But none of his scheming helped Clinton politically.
Even his followers laughed at this new completion
date, saying that the canal could not possibly be completed in their lifetime. In the 1821 election for governor, 180,000 votes were cast. Clinton won by only
2,000 votes.

However, this near defeat could not stop a determined man like Governor Clinton. It only spurred him
to greater effort.

One of the last big problems for the planners to solve
was how to cross rivers and streams. At first they hired
ferryboats to take the horses and drivers aboard and
pull the canal boats across. But this was a very expensive and slow method.

Then they built a few towpaths, like bridges, over
the rivers. But in times of spring floods or summer
drought, even this faster method was unsatisfactory
and often very dangerous. Boats were swept away.
People and animals were drowned and cargo was lost.

So they settled on building aqueducts—expensive
though they were—because they could be depended
upon in all kinds of weather.

Most of the aqueducts were big, uncovered, boxlike
channels built to cross the rivers at the same level as
the canal. They were supported by huge pillars of stone
set in waterproof lime, for they had to carry four feet of
water, a towpath, and the heavily loaded canal boats.
They had to be made of wood, which rotted in time and
needed continual repair. But they worked. Some of

these aqueducts were extremely high so that floods could not wash them away.

Another kind of aqueduct was sometimes built high along the side of a hill, supported by an earthen wall reinforced with stone.

In certain places where expensive aqueducts might have been built, channels were dug around the base of sheer cliffs instead. Then narrow towpaths were carved in the rocks far above. Horses and drivers walked along these high, narrow paths towing canal boats far below on the ends of very long ropes.

More crews were put to work building bridges across the channel, as had been promised the landowners who had donated property for the canal. Every satisfied landowner was a potential voter, the commissioners knew.

These bridges were built as cheaply as possible, which meant that they were as low as possible. That the people riding on canal boats would have to duck every time they went under the hundreds of bridges along the way did not bother the builders at this time. They had more important things to think about.

To fulfill his promise, in the summer of 1823 Clinton announced that the 220-mile channel was open, even though some sections were not actually boatable, and that four beautiful new passenger boats would make regular trips between Utica and Rochester in forty-eight hours.

But the announcement came too late to save Clinton's position as governor. In fact, he had not even been nominated for the position. More important to him at this time, however, he was allowed to continue as president of the canal commission.

De Witt Clinton was a proud and often arrogant man whose blunt manner made many enemies for him. Once he decided to do something, he would listen to no one.

Fortunately for the Erie Canal, he was now obsessed with completing the work before the legislature could stop him, and he devoted all his time to the project.

Poor, because he was working without pay, and limping from the pain of an injury received in early canal days, he traveled from one end of the canal to the other. Doctors often told him he must give up the work, but he would not listen. He directed operations, answered questions, made decisions, and spurred even the newest laborers to greater effort.

To complete Clinton's Ditch in the shortest possible time became the goal of all the people working on it. They pushed the canal seventeen miles farther west. And they opened an eight-mile channel at the extreme eastern end, called the Junction Canal, which brought the Champlain Canal down to Albany.

The time had finally come to solve the riddle of the extreme western section. As yet the place on Lake Erie where the canal should end had not been decided.

Two crude little hamlets on the shore of the lake, Buffalo and Black Rock, were about the same size—little larger than trading posts. Everyone knew that one of these hamlets would be chosen as the canal terminus and would therefore become an important city and a great port. The other would probably remain small and unimportant.

For several years, while the commissioners were unable to make up their minds, the two villages warred with each other. Each owned a rusty old cannon. Whenever a rumor drifted in that one of the villages had been chosen, its citizens fired off its cannon to signal the start of a celebration. Quickly the rival villagers arrived on the scene and a riot broke out. Heads were cracked, noses bloodied, and speech makers shouted down with insults.

After a short period of recovery, another rumor would come along, perhaps that the other hamlet had been chosen. Then war would break out again.

But in midsummer of 1823, the warring ended. The commissioners decided to award the prize to Buffalo. To Black Rock they gave the insignificant job of opening and closing the sluice gates that would let in the lake water.

On the ninth of August everyone in the village of Buffalo and even some of the disgruntled people from Black Rock gathered on a piece of marshland for the ground-breaking ceremony. All who had oxen were asked to bring them. They rigged up a huge plow and hitched it to a dozen yoke of the big, clumsy creatures. With the crack of a whip, the animals moved forward, cutting a deep furrow in the bog between the rows of red stakes.

After that mighty effort, everyone had a drink from the barrels of free whiskey and stood around wondering what to do next. So busy had they been with their wars that no one had thought of how they would carry away the dirt. In the whole village there was not one wheelbarrow or scraper.

But settlers out here in the backwoods had learned to use their imaginations. A few men cut down some trees for poles six to eight feet long and connected two of them at the middle with a crude platform. Others followed their example. Now two men could pile sod onto the platform, lift it by the ends of the poles, and carry it away. They called their clumsy contraptions "soul carts."

As long as the whiskey lasted, a great amount of work was accomplished.

Much of the opposition to Clinton's Ditch had been coming from taxpayers in those areas which the canal did not reach. So Clinton made a sudden decision. He would now take all his workmen off the two difficult ends of the canal and put them to work digging extension canals to three important lakes near the middle section—Seneca, Cayuga, and Onondaga. Thus, he believed, he could open up large new areas to canal transportation and silence many of his critics.

Instead, his decision was just what his political enemies had been waiting for. They used it as an excuse to stage an uproar in the legislature. Both houses voted to dismiss him.

As president of the canal commission, Clinton had been the driving force that kept the work going. Without him, work suddenly came to an end all along the

canal, leaving thousands of men out of jobs. The many
landowners along the right of way, planning enterprises
that would make them rich, were hopelessly stranded.
Many thousands on the eastern coast who were waiting
for the last of those 363 miles of canal to be finished
saw their dreams of migrating shattered in a day.

The combined anger and frustration of these masses
of people turned against the plotters in the legislature.
De Witt Clinton became a martyr—a leader who had
been deposed.

In the spring of 1824 he was again nominated for
governor. This time he was elected by a good majority.
Nothing could stop the completion of Clinton's Ditch
now.

As soon as the ice melted that spring, activity all
along the completed sections of the canal grew enormously. Hundreds of boats filled the waterway, making
it necessary for stronger regulations to be set up.

The year before, when waves were breaking down
the banks at an alarming rate, Clinton had announced a
four-mile-an-hour speed limit and a ten-dollar fine for
exceeding the limit. But now the many different kinds
of boats required different regulations. A slow-moving
barge hauled by a pair of oxen, for example, could not
be allowed to hold back a fast-moving passenger boat
pulled by teams of sleek horses that were changed
every fifteen miles.

One regulation after another was established as the
need arose. But it was some time before a full set of
rules could be drawn up.

First place among the canal boats went to the packets, which carried only passengers and their hand luggage. These were often eighty to ninety feet long, but they were allowed to be no more than eleven feet wide. They must be able to pass other boats with room to spare in the channel that was only twenty-eight feet wide at the bottom.

The main part of the packet was one long room nine feet wide, called the saloon. Because of the very low bridges under which the packet must pass, the saloon had a ceiling so low that passengers could barely stand up. A row of curtained windows along the sides let in some light. In the daytime long tables provided dining space. At night the saloon became the sleeping room.

A tiny galley behind the saloon was the cook's quarters. Here he worked sixteen to eighteen hours a day and slept the few remaining hours at night. At the bow another cubbyhole, called the cuddy, housed the crew.

Outside along both sides were twelve-inch passageways. Above the cabin was the only deck. Here passengers could sit on low-backed benches during the day.

The packets charged the highest fares—three or four cents a mile, depending upon whether or not meals were included.

Next in importance were the emigrant boats, called line boats because one company or line owned fleets of these boats. They were cheap imitations of packet boats and carried people from the East as well as from Europe.

Families with all their possessions, including such things as crates of chickens, crowded onto line boats.

They paid a cent and a half per mile if the captain provided their meals. But many rode for less by taking along their own food. They slept amid fleas and bed-bugs, wherever they could find space in the filthy boats.

Line boats were pulled by tired old horses at the rate of about forty miles a day. Later the canal was referred to as "old cent-and-a-half-a-mile, mile-and-a-half-an-hour" because of these boats. They carried thousands of poor people westward for many years.

At the beginning some freight was carried by the home-designed and home-built boats. But so many of these sank on the first day out that a larger and steadier kind of freighter soon came into use. It carried no pas-sengers—only the captain, his crew, and often his fam-ily.

Since the captain's chief concern was to move as much freight as possible as quickly as possible, he usu-ally carried an extra team of horses on board. One team rested while the other worked.

All the large boats that traveled day and night had headlights called nighthawkers placed on small raised platforms at the prow. They were big lanterns about a foot square with glass on three sides. They burned camphene oil which gave a clear light and did not at-tract insects. The glow from the nighthawkers could be seen for about two hundred feet—far enough so that the driver out ahead with his horses or mules could see any obstructions on the towpath.

Some of the families who moved west chose the cheapest way to go—on their own boats. Since these boats were intended to take the families only to the end of the canal, where they would be abandoned, they were very simple. Often they were little better than rafts with some sort of crude shelters for household goods and protection from rain and wind. The family horse, sometimes helped by men or boys, usually pulled them along. Later, arrangements could be made to rent horses along the way.

Another raftlike type of family boat for which the canal was not really intended was the shanty boat that went nowhere. Owning no land, holding no steady jobs, the shiftless occupants lived out their lives on the canal. They fished, picked up just enough work to pay for a little food, and enjoyed the life that moved past them day and night.

They got in the way of other boats, but at first no one could do anything about them. Later they were forbidden to park in the open channel or within 150 feet of a lock. The only place for them was in a widened area perhaps near feeder canals or town wharves.

The rafts that caused the greatest trouble on the canal were really only piles of logs chained together, called cribs. A number of cribs, sometimes as many as ten, were fastened one behind the other to be pulled along as one unit. But at the locks they had to be separated, passed through one by one, and then fastened together again.

This long process held up traffic and caused much resentment. To avoid riots, the lock-keep sometimes alternated them—one crib and then one boat—easing the resentment only slightly. But logs brought a good price in the East and so were an important part of the commerce from west to east for many years.

In time, different kinds of boats appeared on the canal. Some were traveling stores where groceries and simple household items were sold. Others were the very popular circus boats carrying musical entertainers, acrobats, sleight-of-hand artists, and trained animals to delight the growing canal population.

No two boats on the canal were allowed to have the same name. And every owner was required to register the name and paint it in bold letters on the back of the boat.

As the numbers of boats grew, owners were hard put to find different names for them. Family names often were used for family boats, and when a family expected never to own more than one boat, sometimes more than one name was chosen—like *John and Annie* or *Hattie and Mattie*. A simpler solution was to choose *Four Boys*, or even *Eleven Brothers*.

Some owners may have hoped to smooth their way with *Honest John* or *Fair Play*. Others who considered themselves clever gave their shanty rafts such names as *Palace?* or *Splendid?* And one unschooled boater proudly painted *May Flour* on his craft.

American presidents, signers of the Declaration of Independence, and even such notables as Cleopatra, Napoleon, and Julius Caesar were commemorated. So were some lowly creatures like rats and fleas.

When it came time for a canaller to name the boat he had so lovingly created, his imagination was still working overtime.

5

The Wedding of the Waters

Now that the completion of the Erie Canal was assured and the great benefits for New York were coming to light, neighbors woke up to what was happening. Boston and Philadelphia had been the leading cities in America. Now New York City would quickly surpass them in commerce only because of its new route to the West.

Boston at once thought of cutting a canal to the Hudson River so that it, too, could use the Erie Canal. But a survey showed that in one place 220 locks would have to be constructed in only eighteen miles of canal. A tunnel was considered, instead, but the estimated cost was so high that the Massachusetts legislature gave up the whole idea.

Philadelphia despaired of tying in with the Erie. She would have to send ships by a very roundabout route to

Albany and therefore could not compete. But Pennsylvanians began to push strongly for canals of their own, dreamed up by ambitious though sometimes ill-informed men.

Newspapers printed fantastic stories. One editor in Pennsylvania wrote that Philadelphia could control the whole inland trade of the continent. If only seventy-five miles of canals were built, boats could get to Lake Erie and on through Lake Superior. From there they could quickly arrive at the Columbia River, float down to the Pacific Ocean, and sail on to the Orient. Thousands of people who had no idea of the geography of their country believed him.

A Pennsylvania congressman later suggested that his whole state could be "a congregation of islands" in a vast network of canals. The idea took hold, for the desire for a way west was growing daily.

Even the long route over the Cumberland Road was almost impassable, filled with huge holes and boulders. There was never enough money to maintain it. The first estimate for building it had been thirty thousand dollars. Already the cost was seven million.

Farmers, angry over the burden of taxes for a crumbling road, took out their boiling anger on the road itself. They used rocks from bridges to build cabins on the right of way. They put fences across the road and planted crops on it.

Ohio, which could easily join the Erie Canal at Lake Erie, had already appointed a canal commissioner, a Cleveland lawyer named Alfred Kelley, even though the population was still small and the state was very poor. But the people were so eager for canals that the legislature soon passed an act to authorize them. It employed James Geddes to make a survey now that his work on the Champlain Canal was completed.

Meanwhile, in New York State De Witt Clinton announced that the Erie Canal would be completed on schedule in 1825, even though he had been forced to lose much time. For once, some of the doubters believed him.

Out at Lockport near the western end of the Erie, the amateur engineer Nathan Roberts had been working for several years on a way to get water across the mountain ridge. He finally completed a spectacular plan for a double flight of five locks—one for ascending and one for descending traffic. It would earn for him the title Father of the Lockport Five and would become known as one of the greatest engineering feats in America.

When Clinton saw the design he approved it heartily, and the work was started. Although it had been planned that the locks would be hand-chiseled out of the sheer rock, the cutting was greatly aided by the use of a new product, Du Pont's blasting powder.

Blasters drilled a hole in the rock by hand. Then they filled it almost full with the powder, packed it down with clay, and inserted a fuse of twisted paper. When they lit the fuse they ran as fast as they could. Some did not get far enough away before the blast caught them.

At last towpaths were cut high above the locks, all to be lighted by huge lanterns to guide the horses and drivers along the narrow ledge at night.

While this work was going on, Clinton turned his attention to the last remaining section at the eastern end. Two large aqueducts and twenty-seven locks must be built in a distance of twenty-eight and a half miles. But in spite of the difficulty of the job, the engineers were now so experienced that they completed the work before the first freeze. Water was let into the locks to test them. All worked perfectly.

At the end of 1824, all the tolls for that year on the completed parts of the canal were totaled. Even De Witt Clinton was amazed to learn that nearly one-third of a million dollars had been collected.

Other sources of income were mills that farmers had built where sluice gates regulated water flowing in from feeder streams. The plunging water turned the mill wheels. At first the mill owners paid no fee. But when some legislators realized how much money could have been collected from this source of water power, a tax was imposed.

What the canal would earn when it was opened from end to end was a staggering thought. For all New Yorkers, Clinton's Ditch suddenly became the Grand Canal or sometimes the Grand Western Canal.

Pennsylvania now began plans for building a longer canal system than the Erie. Ohio, with its eyes on the immense tolls, wanted several canals that would tap all parts of the state.

Clinton himself, knowing that the best way to insure his popularity was to keep the taxpayers happy, now turned his attention to a sure system of toll collecting. Early in 1825, while Nathan Roberts was completing his Lockport Five and other engineers were putting the finishing touches on aqueducts and bridges, Clinton had three weighlocks rigged up—at Troy, Utica, and Syracuse. Thus he could catch most of the travelers, for they would have to pass through one or more of these locks.

The first type of weighlock was built so that water could be measured with a boat in it and again after the boat had been floated out. The difference was figured and the toll decided upon.

Soon, however, a better method was invented. The boat floated over a huge cradle, enough water was drained out of the lock to allow the boat to rest on the cradle, and the true weight of the boat was quickly recorded.

Any boat could be weighed in only four minutes. Even so, the locks were busy day and night. Sometimes as many as sixty or seventy boats waited in line to be weighed.

Because of expected business from the canal, New York City had erected thirty-five hundred buildings in 1824. Albany, amazed to learn that its wholesale business had multiplied by four in two years, began a rapid construction program. All the towns and villages along the way prepared themselves for great expansion while their land values boomed.

Impatient almost to the bursting point, the people waited.

In February, 1825, while De Witt Clinton also waited, Ohio called him to officiate at its own ground-breaking ceremony. Earlier he had persuaded John

Jacob Astor to lend the Ohio canal commissioners one million dollars to start operations, and the state was eager to show its gratitude.

Clinton had reasons for wanting to help Ohio. When Ohio canals were completed, traffic to and from New York City would grow tremendously. That traffic would, of course, flow through the Erie Canal, and the tolls collected at the weigh stations would flow into the New York treasury.

Besides, Clinton was now so popular that he was being considered as a candidate for the presidency of the United States. He was more than glad to spread his popularity beyond his home state.

In June the sluice gates at Black Rock were opened, letting in Erie water for the first time. The event was celebrated with the usual noise and hilarity. Lockport too was flooded. But the section between Black Rock and Lockport was not ready for use until the first of October. On that date tolls were first collected at Black Rock.

Meanwhile New York City, which had for so long opposed the canal, realized how wrong it had been. To make amends, it began preparations for the greatest celebration ever known in America.

By late summer it had set up a planning commission that sent out letters to every town and hamlet along the canal and the Hudson River. Explaining that a procession would move down the canal on opening day, they urged each community to outdo its neighbors in preparing a fitting ceremony of greeting.

With all the enthusiasm and talent they could muster, the people set to work. The local schoolmaster or poet was appointed to write an appropriate ode. The town's most important men competed with each other to compose the finest welcoming speeches.

All the others put their talents to work in one way or another. Women wove bunting and dyed it in bright colors for decorations.

Men who had a knack for carving made what they called "illuminations." These were narrow wooden boxes built to any length. Some were long enough to reach all the way across the canal. The men chiseled appropriate phrases through one side of the box. Just before the procession arrived, they would place lighted lanterns inside. The light would shine through the letters to make startling displays along the corridor of the canal.

Such phrases as CLINTON AND THE ERIE or INTERNAL IMPROVEMENTS were popular. Montezuma had the longest illumination. Possibly its builders were unable to decide between the two popular phrases. It read: DE WITT CLINTON AND INTERNAL IMPROVEMENTS.

In some villages, householders agreed to keep candles or lanterns shining through the greased-paper windows of their log cabins during the festivities.

Before dawn on October 26, 1825, a dense crowd had already gathered along the way to the waterfront at Buffalo. At nine o'clock a brass band playing a martial tune set out from the log-cabin courthouse. Then came De Witt Clinton, elegantly attired and wearing a tall beaver hat. He was followed by all the canal commissioners, many other notables, and local committees from towns along the way.

Clinton solemnly took his place at the bow of the *Seneca Chief*, a fine new packet boat built of Lake Erie red cedar and specially outfitted for the history-making voyage. On the side facing the towpath, so that all could see, were two huge oil paintings. One showed the *Seneca Chief* just as she looked at the moment, setting out from Buffalo Harbor. The other painting represented De Witt Clinton himself as Hercules, a mytho logical Greek hero of fabulous strength, dressed in a flowing Greek garment. He was shown standing at rest, having finished his great work of building the Grand Canal.

Also on deck were two brass-bound kegs painted red, white, and blue. These were to be used in a ceremony planned for the end of the journey. One keg was full of water from Lake Erie. The other contained bottles of water supposedly collected from twelve great rivers of the world, including such distant rivers as the Ganges, the Indus, and the Nile. Few in that crowd at Buffalo wondered or cared how the water could have been brought from such a distance in so short a time. But when the story reached envious Philadelphia, there was much scoffing.

In addition, the *Seneca Chief* carried products from the West—potash, flour, butter, and Lake Erie whitefish.

Four other boats made up the flotilla. They carried others of the delegation, more products, and menageries to represent the forest life of the West—animals, fish, and birds. The last, *Noah's Ark*, even displayed two Indian boys.

At exactly ten o'clock, a cannon boomed a signal and the procession moved out, each boat drawn by four matched gray horses. Many other crafts of all colors followed while the crowd cheered and waved.

All along the 523-mile route to New York City Harbor, cannons had been set up within hearing range of each other. Many of the cannons were from Commodore Perry's former ships or had been captured by him from the British on Lake Erie during the War of 1812. Most of them were now manned by war veterans.

As soon as the sound from Buffalo reached the next cannoneer, he fired off his cannon. And so the sound went all down the line, reaching New York City by eleven-twenty.

A grand salute was fired at Fort Lafayette and sent back to Buffalo in the same manner.

Many of the villages along the way existed only because of the canal. A good number—Lockport, Brockport, Newport, and others—had even chosen names to advertise their connection with this important body of water.

Now they tried to show their gratitude in every conceivable way. At most of the villages the procession stopped to listen to odes and speeches, greet the boisterous crowd, consume quantities of food at banquets set up in the largest building available, and witness displays of fireworks. Clinton proudly responded to all the adulation with speeches of his own.

Only Rome and Schenectady refused to join in the celebration. The important merchants of Rome were still miffed over being bypassed by half a mile. The Rome fathers filled a barrel with stagnant water from the abandoned Western Inland Lock Navigation canal, draped it in black, marched as in a funeral procession to the Grand Canal, and emptied the barrel into the new waterway.

Schenectady, too, had considered a funeral procession. It had grown rich as the terminus of the old portage road from Albany. Freight had been loaded there onto river boats, and the owners had profited. Now, the citizens believed, Schenectady would dwindle as freight passed by on Clinton's Ditch to be unloaded at Albany.

New official boats had been added to the flotilla at different stops. *Niagara* was added at Black Rock. *Young Lion of the West* was presented at Rochester with an elaborate formal ceremony. By the time the procession reached Albany, one week after it left Buffalo, its official and unofficial crafts numbered in the hundreds.

At Albany the celebration took on a different character, for this capital of the state was no backwoods village. It had already become a fashionable little city, reveling now in the news that the population had doubled in the past year. Six hundred guests attended an elaborate banquet set up on the Columbia Street Bridge.

The next day the flotilla boats were fastened onto two powerful steamboats for the triumphal ride down the Hudson River. Other boats joined them from every side until the Hudson was covered from shore to shore. More crowds lined the banks all the way.

On November 4, nine days after the first cannon sent its message from Buffalo, what seemed to be the entire population of New York City and thousands of out-of-town visitors were on hand at daybreak to greet the cavalcade when it came into sight. Church bells rang and cannons boomed.

The *Washington*, carrying the Governor's Guard, moved into the stream followed by every boat that would float, crowded to its limit.

"Where are you from and whither bound?" the *Washington* signaled.

"From Lake Erie, bound for Sandy Hook," the *Seneca Chief* replied, as though everyone in the state did not already know.

The *Washington* leading the way, they all set out toward Sandy Hook, New Jersey. There in the harbor the official boats formed a circle, while their hundreds of gaily decorated followers gathered around.

Then Governor Clinton performed the ceremony that everyone had been waiting for, called the Wedding of the Waters. First he poured the keg of water from Lake Erie into the ocean to symbolize the union between the Great Lakes and the Atlantic Ocean. Then a helper poured the bottles of water from the twelve great rivers to show that commerce could now move from all parts of the world through the Erie Canal.

At last Clinton gave a moving speech. This was a triumphant climax for him after all the agony and humiliation he had endured for thirteen years, and he savored every moment of it.

But it was not the end for the assembled crowds. Days of celebrating followed.

A mile and a half of bands headed a giant parade with representatives of every club and organization in the city carrying huge banners or riding in horse-drawn floats.

Copies of the official song were handed out on the streets. It was called "The Meeting of the Waters." Written to commemorate the ceremony, it was dedicated to De Witt Clinton. Although the composer borrowed from an old Irish melody, his words were new and in the usual flowery language of the times. It began:

There is not in the wide world a Valley so sweet
As that vale in whose bosom the bright waters meet;
O the last rays of feeling and life must depart
Ere the bloom of that valley shall fade from my heart.

Let the day be forever remember'd with pride
That beheld the proud Hudson to Erie allied;
O the last sand of Time from his glass shall descend
Ere a union, so fruitful of glory, shall end.

Three stanzas followed, all more elaborate than the first two, and probably more difficult to sing.

When darkness came, a great display of fireworks dazzled the already benumbed thousands.

After the parade came the inevitable banquets—

mammoth ones to match the enthusiasm that the canal had generated. On the last evening the huge ball held at City Hall was lighted by twenty-three thousand candles and lamps. Clinton, now exhausted, fell asleep during the seemingly endless speeches.

Finally the governor and the commissioners were allowed to return to Buffalo. They took along a keg of ocean water to pour into Lake Erie and thus complete the ceremony.

At last the great migration could get underway in earnest. Workers in the East, waiting only for the spring thaw, counted their meager savings and calculated how many acres of prairie land they could buy at the going price of $1.25 an acre. In Europe, the news from New York dramatically stepped up the exodus of jobless poor. Soon the seaports of America were jammed with families ready to settle the West.

Along with the movement of people came a sudden change in freight rates, which dropped from thirty-two dollars a ton for one hundred miles by wagon to one dollar a ton by canal freighter. Thus the new settlers were assured of a market in the East for their furs, timber, grain, and other products. And they knew they would be able to buy, in return, any manufactured goods they would need.

All along the Erie Canal, villages became bustling cities with hundreds of new docks, warehouses, stores, and hotels. The whole project poured undreamed-of money into the treasury of the state of New York and made it the Empire State.

Benjamin Wright

James Geddes

De Witt Clinton

Two views of the Erie Canal at Lockport, New York, show the double flight of five locks that enabled the canal to cross a mountain ridge

Grain boats are towed along a quiet stretch of the canal

On October 26, 1825, the ceremonies for the opening of the
Erie Canal began at Buffalo (above). Nine days later, the
flotilla reached New York City and fireworks lit up City
Hall (top, right). In the harbor at Sandy Hook, New Jersey,
De Witt Clinton poured water from Lake Erie into the
ocean, symbolizing the Wedding of the Waters (bottom,
right)

*Packet boats carry travelers
along the Erie Canal*

6

Hoggees and Towpath Walkers

Now that their work on the Erie Canal was finished, the laborers had to find other jobs. Some, especially large groups of Irishmen and Germans, followed their canal bosses into Ohio. Others went to Pennsylvania to help on a number of smaller canals already underway.

But New York's busy Erie Canal created new jobs that many of these laborers quickly filled. Some helped to build warehouses and docks along the way. Many took jobs in the salt works at Syracuse. Now that markets were available dozens of new companies began extracting salt from the springs, making Syracuse the greatest salt producer in America. Others cut and loaded firewood or filled hundreds of barrels with wood ashes to be sent to the East where they would be used in making lye and soap.

Many of these men settled in the communities permanently. They reared families there and became good and often influential citizens.

The canal itself was an important source of employment, for it needed a crew of twenty-five thousand to keep it operating and to move boats along it.

From the very first, towpath walkers were hired to watch for breaks in the canal and to see that they were repaired quickly. These jobs were usually filled by men who had actually dug and fortified the channel, because they understood the problems that could arise.

Each towpath walker had a certain stretch of canal, usually about ten miles long, that was his special responsibility. Every day, even in storms or intense heat, he walked the full distance watching for anything that might give trouble.

He inspected the locks, aqueducts, and other structures, looking for cracks or signs of erosion. He carefully examined the banks, searching for holes made by the many animals that liked to burrow into them or by men who carelessly rammed their long iron-tipped poles through the clay lining. If he saw a small whirl of water below the surface, which meant that a hole had developed, he quickly waded in, stuffed the hole with a twist of straw, and tamped it with clay.

In places where the animals were especially active, bounties were set up for their capture. As much as fifty cents a head was paid for muskrats and minks caught within eleven yards of a canal. Lesser amounts were offered for those caught farther away. In time, the destructive iron-tipped poles with which boatmen pushed their crafts off sand bars and rocks and guided them into locks were forbidden in the clay-lined channels.

Towpath walkers were on call day and night to help pump out a sinking boat or perhaps to search for a lost child who might have fallen overboard.

Each thirty or forty miles of the canal had its own expert wrecking crew and also a boat called a "hurry-up boat," equipped with picks and shovels, planks and ropes, stakes, straw, clay, and lanterns. These crews took care of major disasters that could come without warning. A lock gate might suddenly break. A part of a bank might cave in. Or, worst of all, a flood from an overflowing stream nearby might wash out a whole section of the canal, including the towpath. When that happened the raging water tossed boats over the berm and out into fields, wrecking the boats, scattering the contents, and killing some of the passengers.

At such times the towpath walker sent a fast horse and rider to summon the wrecking crew.

If a whole section was washed out, the crew drove two rows of tight-fitting piles all across the channel to shut off the canal water from both east and west. Next, they built a new bank by driving two rows of stakes about a foot apart, weaving ropes between them, stuffing the spaces with straw, and tramping it down. When most of the flow of flood water was stopped in this way, the men drove in a full row of strong piling and at last built a new towpath of earth fortified with rock.

Traffic on the canal was stopped for a long time

while this work went on. Boats lined up for many miles.

The Erie Canal was closed for at least three months in the winter. Workmen were hired at this time to clear the channel of sand bars and debris and make major repairs. Unlike other canal workers, the towpath walkers and wrecking crews could thus earn year-round pay.

Another important service on the canal was performed by the locktender, sometimes called a lock-keep. One was stationed at each of the eighty-three locks. Whenever a boat floated into a lock, the tender had to close one huge wooden gate and open the other. He swung the hinged gates open or shut by leaning against a long wooden bar, called a sweep, and walking it around.

The locktender lived in a shack at the lock. His job started with the opening of the canal, usually in March, and ended when ice caused it to be closed, probably late in November. He worked day and night, seven days a week, catching naps whenever he had a few minutes between boats before the long blast of a captain's horn wakened him. When he could no longer stay awake, he simply closed his lock for a few hours, and no amount of tooting could waken him.

Financially, the locktender's job was a good one because he had ways of getting money on the side. In his shack, which became a waiting place for stranded boatmen, he had a bar where he made a profit selling drinks. Sometimes he sold groceries or cures for illnesses: James Fever Powders, Bark and Emetic, or Lee's Anti-Bilious Pills. He kept a large supply of liniments for horses and mules. And he soon learned to give first place to a boatman who slipped him a tip and to hold back others who had failed to tip him on the last run.

Boat captains both hated and feared locktenders. But outwardly they showed them respect, for a locktender could cause a swell that would send a boat on quickly. On the other hand, he could make a boat hit the side of the lock with enough force to damage the hull. He was also treated with respect because he was supposed to settle fights that occurred when two boats claimed first place at his lock. Actually, however, he usually allowed these fights to be settled by fists.

Most of the twenty-five thousand canal jobs were filled by men and boys, and occasionally by women, who in one way or another were attached to the boats that moved up and down the canal.

Large boats usually had a captain, two steersmen, a cook, and sometimes a helper, called a bowsman, who did odd jobs. On small family boats the owner was steersman and his wife was cook. At intervals the wife took over her husband's job while he slept.

The steersman's job was to handle the long wooden tiller at the stern. The tiller directed the huge rudder. Because the boat was towed by horses walking along the towpath, it moved at an angle. The steersman had to work every minute to keep his craft from bumping into other boats, bridges, locks, or the sides of the canal. If he was responsible for any damage, he had to pay a stiff fine. If the boat had to stop for any reason he must jump ashore and fasten it securely.

Steersmen and bowsmen were paid about twenty dollars a month plus food and a place to sleep. If either provided a horse he received another ten dollars.

The drivers of the horses and mules were paid the lowest wages. Adults averaged about twelve dollars a month. Boys were supposed to get ten dollars, but often they were paid only thirty dollars for the whole season. For this reason, boys were usually hired. The only skill required of them was the ability to handle horses.

About ten thousand boys worked as drivers each year on the canal. They were called "hoggees," although no one really knows why. Some say that the term came from old English or Scottish words. Since drivers were constantly calling the directions "Haw" and "Gee" to their animals, the canallers may have combined the sounds for a nickname.

Many of the boy drivers were orphans, some no more than twelve years old, whose parents had died during the terrible trips across the Atlantic in the crowded holds of cargo ships. The boys had been picked up at the docks by canal bosses and hired out to boat owners. Poor, underfed, and ragged, they were looked down upon by the other canallers.

Most hoggees walked in six-hour shifts, swinging a fifteen-foot whip to drive as many as six horses or mules. In their time off they had to feed and care for the animals, mend harnesses, and cook their own food. In the few hours that were left, they could sleep with the horses or mules in the small stables on board. They never had enough sleep.

If they were sick, if cold rain drenched their thin clothes, they were not allowed to stop. Many died of pneumonia or tuberculosis. Only a few ran away, for they had nowhere to go. Those who survived became hardened men at an early age, drinking and fighting for their rights—hoping that some day they might become steersmen and earn twenty dollars a month.

As soon as they were on the job, they had to learn all the rules of the canal, particularly the rules for passing.

Boats going upstream always had the right of way. When two boats met, the hoggee driving the downstream boat had to turn his horses or mules to the outside of the towpath and stop. Then he let his seventy- to ninety-yard towline drop so that it lay flat on the towpath and sank to the bottom of the canal. At the same time, the steersman swung the boat to the far side of the canal to let the upstream boat pass.

The driver of the upstream boat had to keep his towline taut at all times so that it could pass over all other towlines without fouling them. No matter how tired a young hoggee became, he did not dare to relax for a moment. A tangled towline could drag his horses into the canal. Then it was his responsibility to plunge into the water and get the animals to shore. A twelve-year-old hoggee was often no match for a team of frightened, thrashing horses or mules. But if any of the animals drowned, the hoggee knew that he would be beaten by the captain. The animals were more valuable than he was.

When boats were going in the same direction, pack-

ets always had the right of way because they were built
to go faster than any other boats. The driver for a
packet had to be especially skillful because the captain was constantly passing other boats, sometimes
even racing other packets. These races caused many
vicious fights and serious accidents.

No packet went farther east than Schenectady. Because of the many locks between Schenectady and Albany, passengers could get to and from Albany much
quicker by stagecoach.

A good many boys were hired by the packets at
Schenectady as "runners." Their job was to sign up passengers who came in on the stagecoaches. Often when
competition was especially keen, the runners had fierce
fights. For this reason, one area near Schenectady became known as The Battleground.

Men were also hired by the new towing companies
that pulled long strings of canal boats between Albany
and New York City. More worked on Lake Erie between Buffalo and other lake ports. A large crew was
needed to handle the sixty to one hundred canal boats
that were towed by a single steam-powered craft.

For years the Erie Canal and its extensions continued
to provide jobs for many thousands of workers.

7

Life on the Canals

When the first surveyors had gone into the wilderness to set their lines of red stakes, they reported finding families living in crude shelters, often open on one side. Men, women, and children, all longing for sunshine, were struggling to push back the forest and clear places where they could plant a little corn.

If the surveyors' stakes happened to border any of these clearings, life for the families changed at a breathtaking pace as soon as digging began. The clearings quickly became trading posts. When the completed canal brought its stream of traffic, trading posts became towns. Then towns became cities.

A man who had been struggling so hopelessly only a few years before was able to cut his acres into town lots and sell them for thousands of dollars. His lonely wife soon had many neighbors. His children had playmates and in time even teachers.

Before long he built a house of finished lumber and put in real windows of glass manufactured in the East. He ordered china and table linen so that his wife could entertain in the best fashion even though, to reach his door, the guests must still trudge through ankle-deep mud and avoid sprouting tree stumps in the streets. Ignorant as both the husband and wife might be, they joined hastily formed literary societies and listened to concerts and lectures given by traveling entertainers.

All this, they knew, was made possible by the miracle of the canal, and they were grateful for it. So were all the other people of the community, even though many had not been so fortunate as to own canalside land and must still live in log cabins and go barefoot. Their fortunes were changing, too.

For all these people, the arrival of a luxury packet was the highlight of the day. It brought excitement, color, and a glimpse of life from the outside world. At the first blast of a packet horn, everyone rushed down to the wharf to see the matched horses with their silver mountings move to the favored inner side of the towpath and to watch the driver tighten his towline and proudly pass over the lines of all the waiting boats.

Then the people pushed forward to get the best view of the sleek packet as it raced up at four miles an hour.

The packet brought the mail, some newspapers from the East, and gossip. And on its deck was the best show in town. Ladies sat on the low-backed benches holding frilled parasols to keep the sun from darkening their delicate skin. Their bustles stood out at the correct angle, and their draped skirts, modestly covering their ankles, gave only a glimpse of dainty shoes.

Many a canalside girl, seeing the fashion parade, looked down at her brown ankles above her bare feet and tried to cover them with the hem of her mud-stained skirt.

The men, too, came in for scrutiny. They lounged about in their fitted pearl gray coats, their tall hats, and their tapered trousers strapped under their insteps. They wore ruffled white shirts that soon won them the nickname "Ruffleshirts."

These gallants from the East stood out sharply from the canallers who, dressed for comfort, wore wide pantaloons held up by bright-colored suspenders. Their short boxed coats and shirts were made of homespun wool. In cold weather they put on ear muffs.

But traveling on the luxury packets was not as glamorous as it seemed to be from the wharves.

Many of the early travelers were people on a tour of the country, for western New York State was as foreign to most Easterners as was Europe. Europeans, sometimes with their families, came over to explore as though they were going to the heart of Africa.

The tourists found some of what they were looking for—the quiet beauty of the deep forest, the spectacular views from high aqueducts, the novelty of going through the locks, especially the Lockport Five. They

saw multitudes of colorful birds, and animals so tame
that they came to the canals to drink and stare at the
passing show.

At first, especially, they enjoyed the quiet movement
of the boat—so different from the bone-jarring trip
from Albany to Schenectady by stagecoach. The packet
glided along as if on air. Only the frequent cries of
"Low bridge—everybody down" marred the tranquil
ride. For then all on the deck must drop to the floor to
avoid having their heads crushed as they went under a
bridge.

But after a few days the trip became tedious, and the
swarming insects made life miserable. Ladies wore veils
over their bonnets and fanned themselves constantly.
Men put on heavy cloaks, even in sweltering weather.
Still, whining mosquitoes found tender flesh, took sips
of blood, and left red, stinging marks.

As the desire to travel increased, packets began to
take on too many passengers—often two or even three
times as many as they were built for. This practice created incredible problems, particularly at night.

After the supper tables were cleared, the process of
getting people bedded down began. Bowsmen pushed
the tables and benches to the center of the saloon. Then
they attached three or four tiers of shelves all along the
sides of the room and supported them with ropes or
chains. These shelves were twelve inches wide, the top
one only about eight inches from the ceiling. On each
shelf the bowsmen placed a thin pallet, a rumpled
sheet, and a skimpy blanket.

In some of the best packets, a curtain was pulled across a small portion of the forward part of the saloon. This was to shut off a section for the ladies and give them the illusion of having their own quarters. But every sound could be heard through the curtain.

When all was ready, the captain strode into the crowded saloon carrying the passenger list. He read off a few names and went outside again until those passengers whose names had been read had taken their places on their assigned shelves.

The ladies removed their bonnets and shoes and loosened their corsets. Most of the men took off their boots, hats, and coats. But otherwise few made any attempt to undress. They could see that they would scarcely be able to move once they got themselves into place. They could not turn over without falling off. They could not raise their heads without cracking them on the shelf or ceiling above. Worst of all, they had to get onto those shelves while the other passengers watched, commented, and laughed hilariously—especially when a fat man tried to get onto a top shelf.

One English writer and traveler, Charles Dickens, wrote of how he solved his problem. ". . . my shelf being a bottom one, I finally determined on lying upon the floor, rolling gently in, stopping immediately I touched the mattress, and remaining for the night with that side uppermost, whatever it might be. Luckily, I came upon my back at exactly the right moment."

The last passengers were given places on tables and benches, and even under the tables.

When all were bedded down the lamps were turned low, and then the noise seemed to increase. Every few minutes the captain blew his horn, loudly demanding his right to pass other boats. The crew tramped back and forth on the deck only a few inches from the top bunks.

People banged their heads against the ceiling or the shelf above and moaned loudly. Children cried. Men snored in every key.

One after another, passengers gasping for breath in the stifling saloon struggled out of their berths and staggered toward the door. In the darkness they stumbled over outflung arms and legs, wakening some who had been fortunate enough to fall asleep. The curses that followed them wakened others who answered in kind.

Since no one was permitted to sleep on deck, the exhausted wanderers finally stumbled back to their pallets, followed by another storm of insults.

Mr. Dickens complained about the American practice of spitting. It seemed to grow worse at night and was accompanied by loud snuffling and throat-clearing.

Meanwhile, mosquitoes feasted on the captives.

After a night of torture the traveler was turned out of the saloon so that it could be made ready for breakfast. He staggered up onto the deck where he could take his turn in line to dip murky canal water into the tin washbasin, splash some of it onto his puffy face, and perhaps use the comb that was fastened onto a chain nearby. Then he could jump to the towpath and take a brisk walk.

When the cook beat on a pan to call him to breakfast, he hurried to the next low bridge, dropped onto the deck as the packet passed under it, and went below.

The saloon, now fitted with long tables and benches, was still stuffy with the odor of many sweating bodies. But the food on the tables was plentiful and usually very good. By some miracle, from his tiny galley the cook had produced great platters of several kinds of fried meats and fish, large dishes of pickles and puddings, loaves of fresh bread, mounds of butter, pitchers of hot tea, and plenty of maple syrup and honey to pour over everything. All the passengers helped themselves until the platters were bare.

Twice more—at noon and toward evening—bountiful meals were served. These consisted of several kinds of roast meat and game, fresh vegetables, and assorted pies and cakes.

All this was included in the price of the fare, now about four cents a mile but occasionally five cents.

When a traveler wanted a change from the torture of the crowded packet, he could spend a night or two in one of the hastily built taverns along the way and then take a later boat. For a shilling (twelve and a half cents) he could have space on a tavern bed with any number of strangers. One tavern keeper, according to legend, waited until a lodger was sound asleep and then moved him to the floor and rented his space to another for an additional shilling.

The daytime boredom on a packet could be relieved in a number of ways. While the boats waited at locks or stopped at town wharves to pick up or deliver pas-

sengers and take on supplies, the ladies strolled along
the boardwalks, pretending not to hear the rough language while they listened to canalside talk. They
dropped in at canal shops and sometimes bought articles that they needed—combs, or perhaps skeins of
embroidery thread.

The men had a much greater number of diversions to
choose from. They could visit one of the circus boats or
try their luck at a game of chance at a carnival stall.
Those with plenty of money, or hoping to make some,
were always ready to bet on anything that moved, from
two boys wrestling beside the towpath to two cater-
pillars creeping slowly out of a chalk-drawn circle.

When the four-miles-an-hour pace of the packet became intolerably slow, the dandies on board took up a
collection and urged the driver to whip up his horses. If
the pace was still not fast enough, the men jumped off
the boat, grabbed the towline, and raced along with it.
At the head of the line at the next stop, they gladly paid
the ten-dollar fine while the driver kept the horses moving.

A good number of the packet passengers were land
speculators. In newly opened settlements like Buffalo
and Rochester they worked quickly. They knew all the
tricks of getting land at low prices and selling it at high
prices to green immigrants who had been convinced
that they were getting bargains. Often the speculators
needed no cash at all to make a deal. They passed land
deeds from one person to another so fast that cash from
a buyer could be used to pay the original owner while
the speculator pocketed the profit.

Professional gamblers too rode all the packets, often passing themselves off as wealthy Easterners who had business to conduct in the West. During the long hours of travel they casually mentioned games of cards, pulled out marked decks, and relieved unwary passengers of quantities of money.

Because of the gambling and the great amount of drinking that went on along the canal, many missionaries rode the packets. They persuaded captains to allow them to conduct long prayer meetings in the crowded saloons. And for a while they succeeded in halting all travel on the canal on Sundays.

But the boat owners objected strenuously to losing a profitable day. And the bored travelers simply used the time for hunting, gambling, and even more drinking. Crewmen, accustomed to a hard and active life, turned to fighting as a diversion. So in time the ban on Sunday travel was lifted.

In fact, the missionaries were seldom able to curb the swearing, drinking, and fighting. As traffic grew heavier and more boats competed for first place at the locks, fighting grew fiercer. Every crewman was intensely loyal to his boat and always ready to defend its place in the line with his fists. Few were above cutting towlines to get revenge.

No canal rules were as strong as heavy blows from a canal bully. And with whiskey at only six and one-fourth cents a quart, any canal worker, even the poorest young hoggee, could become roaring drunk and take on someone twice his size.

Freighters were often floating homes for the captain

and his family—the only homes that they knew for many years.

The wife had her special domain at the stern, a tiny space that she made as homey as possible. She hung bright curtains at the small windows and kept flowers blooming in cans on the windowsills.

Since the space was too small for cooking, her stove stood on the rear deck. At mealtimes, the delicious odor of frying potatoes and onions caused many a hungry hoggee to turn his head and take a deep sniff. Even during a rainstorm she cooked on the outdoor stove while one of the children held an umbrella over the sputtering skillet. In her spare moments, after she had washed the clothes in water dipped from the canal and had hung them on lines strung across the cargo-filled deck, the wife also took over some of her husband's work.

Children played all over the barrels and crates on board. Whenever some freight was unloaded and cargo was added, a favorite game of hide-and-seek had new and exciting routes and hide-outs.

Almost before they could walk, boys learned to swim in the shallow water. In fact, much of their time was spent in the muddy channel where they devised all sorts of ways to enjoy themselves. Sometimes they lay on their backs, feet against the bow, while the boats pushed them along. Sometimes they hung onto the rudder and each other, a long chain of naked bodies wiggling and shouting as they were drawn effortlessly along.

When they grew tired of these games they made boats out of wood chips and sailed them for hours, arguing over whose chip boat could best ride the swells from passing crafts.

Freight captains without families often hired only one helper, thus keeping down the cost of running a boat. The two men took turns at steering and driving. The man who held the tiller managed to do it with one hand while he cooked with the other. He gulped his meal from the skillet while he worked. Then he jumped off and took the place of the driver who rushed back to the stern. There he too worked with one hand and ate with the other. Any washing up had to be done, somehow, in the brief moments when traffic was halted, perhaps to make way for a fast packet. And sleep was taken in snatches whenever the boat had to wait at a dock or lock.

The crowded, filthy line boats moving at their slow pace of a mile and a half an hour were miserable places on which to live during the long trip west. And yet their passengers probably complained less than any others on the canal.

To those who had endured long weeks of seasickness in the holds of emigrant ships, a chance to move quietly along and to breathe fresh air was a welcome change. And the fact that they were at last nearing the western paradise for which they had been longing was reason enough for contentment.

People from the same countries of Europe gathered together to exchange experiences and details about the land to the west. In Swedish, Dutch, French, or German, as well as in English, they argued the advantages of settling in the Ohio country or going on to Indiana, Illinois, Missouri, or Michigan territory. Always they talked of their fears that the best land would be taken, that there could not possibly be enough land for all who were migrating.

Often before the line boats reached Buffalo, families from the same country had already made plans to stay together, found colonies somewhere, and in time persuade relatives and friends from the old country to join them. And Easterners, filled with glowing accounts that they had heard in booming towns along the way, were ready to send wildly enthusiastic letters back home, just as soon as they had found their own plots in paradise.

Usually it took a washout or a broken lock to bring all the people together. During the long wait for repairs, line boaters talked with freight boaters and family boaters. And all talked with tavern owners, shopkeepers, dockworkers, and farmers. For all these people had something in common—they had left their homes behind them. Once they had turned their eyes to the West, they would not look back.

8

Ohio Waterways

While Pennsylvania and other eastern states were frantically trying to revive some of their old short-line canal projects, Ohio moved quickly ahead with its plans to bring in settlers and improve its economy by building canals.

Alfred Kelley, who had given up his law practice in Cleveland to work as canal commissioner for only three dollars a day, became so dedicated to his work that he was soon called the De Witt Clinton of Ohio. With unswerving determination he moved each project forward in spite of grave problems that would have defeated a lesser man.

Once it had been decided that Ohio should have canals, every section of the state wanted one. An early idea to satisfy as many people as possible was to dig one long canal diagonally across the state from northeast to southwest connecting Lake Erie with the Ohio River. But that route would not do, for it ignored the two most important elements—an adequate water supply along the way and the levelest route possible.

Meanwhile, James Geddes spent eight months directing surveys of every probable route. He found five that were possible. But Ohio could not afford to build so many. Actually it could not afford to build any.

However, in February, 1825, the legislature passed a law creating a board of seven canal commissioners and a canal fund. It approved the borrowing of money and authorized two canals.

One of these canals, called the Ohio and Erie, was to run through the most thickly populated part of the state from Cleveland on Lake Erie to Portsmouth on the Ohio River. To satisfy people in this eastern section, however, the channel was to meander from one town to another. This was a very expensive way to build a canal, but almost everyone from the governor down to the poorest farmer approved the route. For, as the governor explained and every farmer knew, it cost more to haul a load of produce twenty-five miles over poor roads than the load was worth.

It had already been proved in New York that canals would dramatically reduce freight rates for the producers. And tolls would soon provide huge sums for the state. So why should anyone worry?

A second, shorter canal—called the Miami—was authorized to run sixty-six miles from Cincinnati by way of Hamilton and Middlesex to Dayton along the Miami

River in southwestern Ohio, with the promise that later it would be extended to Lake Erie.

And so it was that Governor De Witt Clinton attended the ground-breaking ceremonies in Ohio on July 4, 1825, three months before the Erie Canal was officially completed.

Governor Morrow of Ohio met him at Cleveland and took him by stagecoach to Newark on a road lined with cheering citizens. Three miles out of Newark, at Licking Summit, ten thousand people were assembled for the most important occasion the young state of Ohio had yet known.

De Witt Clinton, the miracle man, was the chief attraction. Tall, handsome, dignified—and by now well acquainted with the proper procedures at official ceremonies—he lifted the new spade decorated with flowers and turned the first spadeful of dirt. Governor Morrow was next. Then other dignitaries staged a most undignified scuffle to be third.

When it was time for Clinton to speak to the crowd, he predicted a future for Ohio that made his listeners' heads spin. After an exuberant introduction, he went on:

> . . . your sister states, and the civilized world, will be astonished. It [Ohio] will exhibit a spectacle, unprecedented and amazing. An infant wielding the club of Hercules, and managing the lever of Archimedes with irresistible power. When the eagle, in its first flight from the aerie soars to the heavens, looks at the sun with an unfailing eye, and bears in its talons the thunderbolts of Jove, who will not admire this sublime sight.

Only a few had any idea who Hercules and Archimedes were, but they were all convinced that soon Ohio would be the grandest place in the whole world, even though at the moment they did not have two coins to jingle together in their pockets. Thus Clinton secured for himself a large block of political supporters.

The celebrations continued for nearly a month. The whole party traveled west on horseback through the forests to the Miami Canal site, where rousing festivities were held in three villages. Then back they went to the southern part of the Ohio and Erie Canal route, where towns and villages vied with each other in noise and illuminations all along the way north.

At last Clinton returned to New York to supervise the final work on his own Erie Canal and to prepare for the October opening.

Work on the Miami Canal began at once. In spite of spring floods the next year, which made many repairs necessary, water was turned into the canal in 1827, just two years after it was begun.

But to everyone's horror, the water did not fill the channel. It simply soaked into the porous soil. By winter, enough had collected to float a few boats. Then it was closed to let the earth settle.

The next year water stayed in the channel and boats ran all the way from Cincinnati to Dayton. By 1830, locks to carry the water down the 112 feet to the Ohio River were finished.

A packet company built elegant boats for this short

canal in the backwoods. They were painted white and had awnings for the decks. The horses wore bells and ribbons.

The interiors were fitted out with red silk curtains, fine upholstery, and comfortable bunks. On the sixty-six-mile run from Dayton to Cincinnati, passengers were served five delicious meals. Between meals, those who were not too full to move danced on the top deck to the music of a fiddler.

Meanwhile a two-mile canal around the treacherous falls on the Ohio River at Louisville, Kentucky, had been built. So now southwestern Ohio was open to trade on the lower Ohio River and all the way to New Orleans on the Mississippi.

Perhaps more important, those settlers who had reached this backwoods area by hard travel along Indian trails could now easily and safely move on by water if they wished.

The Ohio and Erie Canal started more slowly. Engineers brought from the Erie Canal were not experimenting now. They laid the groundwork carefully, taking every advantage of existing water supplies and topography.

Near the summit, housing was put up for the experienced Irish and German workmen who would construct the stone locks, working for thirty cents a day plus their meals. Their group of shanties was the beginning of the town of Akron.

To cut down on lock and aqueduct building, the canal was planned along stream beds wherever possible, especially if they were in clay soil that would hold water.

Much of the right of way was public land only recently taken from the Indians and therefore free to the state for canal building. Bordering farmers were very generous in giving the canal company marshy land near streams—of little use to them anyway. Besides, they received four to five dollars an acre in advance for clearing the land they had donated.

Since the big timber was on higher ground, the farmers, their sons, and their farm hands had to do little more than grub out the cattails and underbrush and cart them away. They could work in their spare time, live at home, and receive real money, which they seldom saw otherwise. However, they sometimes had to cut down trees, for one rule was that all timber must be cleared twenty feet back from the channel to avoid the danger of trees falling across the waterway.

The decision to cut canals through marshy land along stream beds brought on terrible problems that the engineers should have anticipated. With the coming of warm days in 1826 came the mosquitoes. They brought the malaria that had killed thousands in the Montezuma swamps in York State.

Ohio canals were farther south than New York canals. They were warmer; the mosquitoes remained for a longer time. Few workmen escaped what they called the shakes or the agur or agy, and many died.

Again the only prescribed remedy was whiskey,

brought around in pails and doled out every five hours day and night. It did no good except to keep the workmen in a dulled state, less aware of their condition.

The whiskey and the malaria both slowed down the work. Still, new workers were always waiting to take the places of those who were too sick to work or who had died. Meanwhile, no one even thought of giving up. During 1826, thirty-five thousand workers were employed on the Ohio canals.

At first the canal commissioner, Alfred Kelley, thought the swamp sickness would not last long. With all his experienced help, he should see the canals completed in a short time, he believed.

But in spite of real progress during that first year, the "mud and the mire" of the swamps and the constant turnover of workers because of the fevers made the digging drag on and on.

After the first year, James Geddes accepted a call from Pennsylvania to supervise a survey. Many experienced workers also went to Pennsylvania where they could make better wages and possibly escape the sickness. Before long Ohio was short of workers, and wages had to be raised.

As each section of the canals was opened, the citizens staged magnificent celebrations like those that had been staged all along the Erie Canal. They had reason to celebrate, for the freight rates dropped greatly as new markets became available.

But since the farmers could now make more money

shipping their produce out of the state, they saw no reason to supply the canal contractors at the same low prices as before. So the higher cost of provisions was added to the higher wages, and the state had to come up with more money.

The brunt of the problems fell upon Alfred Kelley. Like De Witt Clinton before him, he went from one trouble spot to another along the canals. Often sick and usually near exhaustion, he ignored the intense heat of summer and the biting cold of blizzards in winter. All the while, he continued to explain the financial needs to the legislature and press for more money.

Fortunately, in 1828 the Congress of the United States made grants of federal land to several states to aid them in building canals. Ohio received five hundred thousand acres of land which it could sell for money to extend the Miami Canal up to the Maumee River, the only truly navigable river in Ohio, which flowed into Lake Erie. The state was required to begin work on the Miami extension within five years and complete it within twenty.

Heartened by this windfall, Commissioner Kelley pushed himself even harder. When the originally authorized canals were at last nearing completion, he was so weak that he had to remain in bed while he continued to supervise the work.

That last year, 1832, was tragic not only for Ohio but for the whole country. Since 1816, an epidemic of Asiatic cholera had been moving from India across Europe, carried by travelers from one country to another.

With the increase in the number of filthy emigrant ships that crossed the Atlantic, it was only a matter of time until the dreaded disease would travel to the New World.

Early in 1832, one of those ships loaded with dead or dying cholera victims landed in Quebec. Passengers still alive frantically sought help from the Canadians and thus quickly spread the disease. Other infected ships followed and moved up the St. Lawrence River to Montreal. There, too, hundreds of citizens died within a few hours or days, often having no idea what caused their death.

Cholera was like no other disease then known. It struck suddenly with little warning. A person in good health in the morning would begin to have a feeling that something was wrong. Soon he seemed consumed with an internal fire that no amount of cold water would satisfy. Within an hour or two he collapsed in agony from stomach spasms that were quickly followed by general weakness and cold. Before night he was dead.

Since people traveled chiefly by canals, the cholera moved along the canal routes. It flowed down the Champlain Canal to Albany and quickly raced along the Erie. Clinton's Ditch became one long scene of horror.

Over many of the villages and towns hung a thick pall of smoke and a sickening stench. Buckets of tar were burned and vats of lime were kept boiling day and night, supposedly to purify the air.

People ran frantically through the dim streets crying out for doctors for stricken members of their families. Death carts rattled from one street corner to another to pick up bodies stacked there. Gravediggers received two dollars for each corpse they buried, but few people were willing to do the work at any price.

Since the canal was blamed for bringing the scourge, traffic was stopped at the edge of many towns. But it would have stopped anyway, for by that time the disease had already slipped in and killed locktenders, towpath walkers, hoggees, tavern keepers, and many others whose business had been to keep the canal traffic alive.

In addition to the canals, many other things were believed to be the cause of the disease. Bad air, fumes from the earth, insects too small to see, indigestible vegetables, pork, watermelons, and strawberries were only a few of the many things that doctors listed.

One doctor suggested that to avoid getting the disease people should put their feet in hot ashes and water and then cover up in bed with hot bricks and boiled ears of corn, drink warm mint tea, and put mustard poultices on their stomachs. But before they could make all those preparations, they were often too sick or were dead.

A few doctors talked about the lack of personal cleanliness and the need for a good, sensible diet. They recommended, among other things, that people clean the streets, air their rooms, and take baths daily.

However, no one seriously considered the idea of isolating the sick. Most people simply used their own ideas of what to do, relying on customs brought from the old country.

Soon the cities of New York, Philadelphia, and Baltimore were stricken. So was the village of Chicago.

Cholera relentlessly moved on to Ohio, Indiana, Illinois, and Michigan territory. Finally it reached all the way down the Mississippi River to New Orleans, taking one out of every six people there in twelve days.

The dreaded disease did not wait for the Ohio canals to be completed. In August, 1832, it arrived at Cleveland, Ohio. By October it found its way to Cincinnati, down on the Ohio River, and killed 301 people in three weeks.

Meanwhile, work stopped all along the Ohio canals and people fled in terror. Only the frosts of winter ended the cholera for the year. In 1833, it came again but in a milder form in most areas. In 1834, it returned once more. And then it slowly died out.

As soon as the first wave of cholera began to slow down, migration from east to west resumed. Once families were on their way, there was no turning back. No one wanted to settle where the disease could strike again. Even while they buried their dead, they were anxious to move on. Surely someplace out west was free of the plague, if only they could live to find it.

Those workers who were left at the Ohio canal sites went back to finishing the locks, aqueducts, bridges, and towpaths. On January 22, 1833, the canal commissioners announced that the two canals, authorized eight years before, were finished.

Now, with money from the sale of the federal lands granted to them, they were ready to begin the extension of the Miami Canal to the Maumee River. This stretch required many expensive aqueducts. Besides, the engineers decided to make it ten feet wider than the first section, thus adding to the cost and the time required to finish it.

The final section, sixty-nine miles along the Maumee River to Toledo on Lake Erie, was also very difficult to build but for a different reason. Much of it had been an old trail through the Black Swamp—the earliest route into the Mississippi Valley after the French had settled in Indiana and Illinois. It was then known as "the road with a tavern every mile" because travelers who were constantly being stuck in the spongy mud needed taverns in which to spend many nights along the way.

The channel through the Black Swamp was made sixty feet wide and six feet deep, but at times, because of the spongy character of the land, the river itself was used—entered by what were known as side-cuts.

The canal was not completed all the way from Cincinnati to Lake Erie until 1845. By that time the name had become the Miami and Erie Canal.

Laborers on this canal through wilderness areas were well paid. Since the new land was cheap, many of them bought plots of it and settled along the route.

In a number of ways, the Ohio canals were different from New York's Erie Canal, chiefly because Ohio had profited from New York's experience. Those sections that were built later and were wider set a trend toward widening all the earlier canals.

The locks themselves were more substantial. The walls were built of stone and were very thick—five feet at the bottom and four feet at the top. They were neatly put together—the blocks of stone carefully cut and fitted and everything made to exact specifications. Wooden floors were built into all the locks. They were made of solid white oak cut one foot thick, laid lengthwise. Over this, three-inch planks were laid crosswise.

Basically, aqueducts were like those on the older Erie Canal—built on arches or pillars of stone. Most of them, as in New York, used wood for the channel itself. But in Ohio it was the custom to enclose them and build roofs over them in order to protect them from rotting.

The gates, aqueducts, and any other parts that had to be built of wood were all painted a soft, deep red color —barn red, sometimes called Indian red. Soon people planted sycamore trees along the raw gash in the land. When the yellow stone and red wood weathered and the trees sent out their fresh green leaves, the canals were very attractive.

Frequently the canals entered large basins of water, called widewaters. These were not planned originally, but occurred in areas where so much water accumulated that it could not be drained off or channeled into a reservoir.

These widewaters proved to be very convenient

places in which boats could turn around or take on or discharge cargo. Boat owners could arrange to store their boats in one or another during the winter.

Pleasant communities grew up along the widewaters. Warehouses, stores, taverns, and homes clustered there —most of them painted white. In summer, people anchored small boats in front of their green-shuttered homes. In winter, they skated on the smooth surface of the ice.

Communities also grew up where locks clustered together. The locktenders had their houses, barns, and stores. Millers constructed their grist mills where they could take advantage of the water power. Blacksmiths put up shops for shoeing the animals that pulled the boats and stables for housing them. Others built stores, workshops, and homes nearby.

Aware of New York's mistake of building bridges too low, Ohio built hump-backed bridges, high enough in the middle so that passengers did not have to drop to the floor whenever their boats went underneath.

These bridges, like the main streets of small towns, became gathering places for the villagers. People hung over the railing to watch the boats go by, to sell eggs or fresh vegetables to the cook, or to recommend taverns. But especially they asked about news up and down the canal. For here too canal boats were the only links with the outside world.

The canal boats themselves were usually more attractive. They were all painted white and the packets had green shutters at the windows which could be closed when passengers needed to be shielded from the prying eyes of the villagers, especially when they were being "locked through." Even the living quarters on freight barges, including kitchens built inside, were equipped with green shutters.

The Ohio canals did not run the usual line boats. The freighters took care of the poorer people who were forced to travel at the cheapest rate.

At first some freight boats owned their own fleets of horses or mules that they stabled at relay stations. Thus they could change animals at regular intervals and not have to drive them until they were worn out. Later, to save money and time, they stabled their extra animals in the middle of their boats or barges, although a few had their stables in the forward part. They let down platforms something like drawbridges for the horses or mules to walk over to go to or from the towpath.

Because mules were usually hard to handle, a custom grew up on the Miami and Erie Canal to put large round blinders on them. These stood out at an angle and gave the appearance of huge eyeglasses.

The Ohio and Erie Canal was 309 miles long, and the Miami and Erie, when entirely completed, ran for 248 miles. The combined length was about one and a half times the length of the Erie Canal.

Because the canals ran from north to south, they did not help very much in moving people farther west. But Ohio *was* the West for many of the travelers. It was on the far side of the mountains where they had longed to go. They settled on the rich land and increased the population enormously—soon placing Ohio third on the list of most populous states. The two canals made it possible for them to sell their produce for a good price, and most of them were content.

But some families, now that they had made the first big move, still turned their eyes westward, wondering what was out there in all that vast land. Some day they would have to find out.

Boats on the Miami and Erie Canal unload at Cincinnati

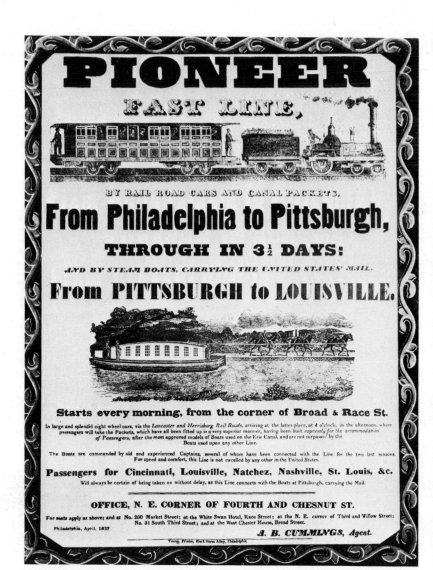

One of the original posters advertising the Pennsylvania Canal (above). At right, a view of the Portage Railway between Johnstown and Hollidaysburg. Attached to strong cables, cars were lifted and then lowered over the Allegheny mountain ridge on ten inclined planes

A barge glides along a stretch of the Pennsylvania Canal

On the *Whitewater Canal* (above), a boat passes the home
of William Henry Harrison at North Bend, Ohio; in the
foreground is a steamer on an inlet of the Ohio River.
(Below) *The Illinois and Michigan Canal*, last of the era,
brought prosperity to Chicago

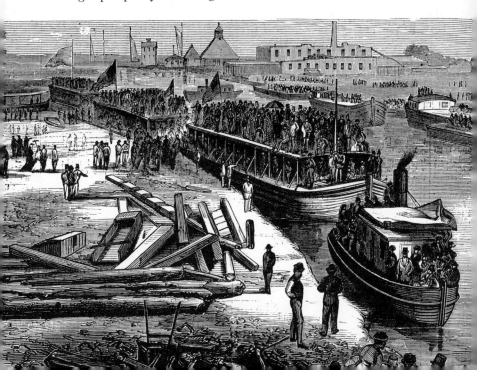

The growing popularity of railroads put an end to the canal era. Here, an engine pulling many freight cars crosses the Erie Canal in upper New York State about 1865

9

Pennsylvania's Grand Canal

By the time New York was preparing to honor De Witt Clinton and his Erie Canal, Philadelphians were thoroughly agitated. New York City was showing definite signs of tremendous growth only because its state had managed to open a waterway to the West. Soon the city would surpass Philadelphia in population and wealth if something was not done.

There was no question about it—Pennsylvania must have its own route west, and very soon, too, before the Erie Canal became established and developed as the main route.

After all, men argued, Philadelphia was only half as far from the heartland of Ohio as was New York City. If a canal were routed in a direct line westward across the state to Pittsburgh and then north to Lake Erie, canal boats would be able to make the trip in half the time. They could cut freight rates in half for the farmers and entice many of the people clamoring to go west who otherwise might go by way of the Erie.

The revenue from tolls would become enormous and quickly pay off any debt for construction that the state would incur. The tolls could even support the whole state and pay the cost of education for all the children. Soon New York City would be returned to its former less important position, and Philadelphia would take first place in the country. So men talked and dreamed.

A board of three canal commissioners had been appointed in 1824. In February, 1825, during the month when the Ohio legislature passed the act to authorize canals, the Pennsylvania board belatedly made its report.

Although one member did not agree, two of the members stated that a canal from Philadelphia to Pittsburgh was "perfectly practicable." To silence all questions about how they expected to carry a canal over mountains nearly twenty-three hundred feet high, they recommended that a tunnel be dug under the mountains. For the benefit of those in the legislature who did not know what a tunnel was, they explained that it was a "hole like a well dug horizontally through a hill or a mountain."

This simple explanation for the tremendous engineering feat that they were proposing seemed to satisfy many who were so eager for a way west that they would believe anything.

People in the northeastern and southern parts of

Pennsylvania who could not directly benefit from the proposed canal objected strongly. So did the owners of turnpikes and taverns and fleets of freight wagons who would lose their means of making a living. Others who believed that horse-drawn railroads were the answer to the problem added their voices. They could build a railroad from Philadelphia to Pittsburgh in one-third the time and at one-third the cost, they insisted.

But they were shouted down by the canal advocates of the two big cities. Canals were democratic because anyone could use them. Railroads were not.

Copying De Witt Clinton's successful method, citizens of Philadelphia prepared a memorial to the legislature urging that water communication be quickly opened all the way to Lake Erie. They organized public meetings all over the state and obtained great numbers of signatures on copies of the memorial.

When they presented all the signed copies to the legislature, the lawmakers were forced to take action. They appointed a new board of five commissioners to hire engineers and draftsmen and to come up with a plan for financing the work.

Meanwhile, a few men objected on a sound basis. The proposed Pennsylvania canal would need four to five times as many locks as the Erie Canal had, and these must be built through the high, rocky mountains. As one newspaper editor wrote: "We will certainly fail to compete with the State of New York for the trade of the West. Nature has given her advantages which we cannot overcome."

But reasonable voices too were drowned out. A bill

passed the legislature on February 25, 1825. It provided for the construction of the canal at the expense of the state and gave it a name—the Pennsylvania Canal, although it was soon referred to as the Grand Canal. It was the only canal ever authorized to compete with the Erie Canal.

James Geddes came from Ohio; Nathan Roberts and Canvass White joined him. Thus Pennsylvania had the services of the best engineers developed by the Erie. It also had in its favor about nine years of American progress which had produced greater supplies of tools and other equipment and more experienced workmen. Unlike the wilderness area of York State in which the engineers had begun to develop their skills and knowledge, Pennsylvania was well populated.

The ground-breaking ceremony took place at Harrisburg where a part of the canal could easily be dug in both directions alongside the Susquehanna River. The usual elaborate ceremony of fireworks and speeches on July 4, 1826, followed the pattern set nine years earlier at Rome, New York, and one year earlier at Licking Summit in Ohio.

Pennsylvanians fully expected to pass up backwoods Ohio in a short time and complete their Grand Canal quickly.

The three engineers worked together on the problems of the route that had been decided upon. What they finally created was a marvel of engineering for its time.

They soon saw that it would be impossible to build

the usual kind of canal all the way. On two stretches—
the first, 172 miles long from Columbia to Hollidaysburg, and the other, 104 miles long from Johnstown to
Pittsburgh—regular canals could be dug although they
would require many more locks than the whole Erie
Canal had needed. But the engineers had to figure out
some other way of getting passengers and freight over
the remaining 118 miles.

A thirty-five-mile tunnel through the Alleghenies, as
had been originally suggested, was an impossible idea.
But a railway on an inclined plane, on which cars
would be drawn up one side and let down the other by
mechanical means, seemed to be the answer.

Canvass White was put in charge of planning and
building this inclined plane, which would be called the
Portage Railway.

On the hilly stretch west of Philadelphia they would
have to build a railway on which horses would draw
the cars most of the way, they decided. In spite of all
the arguments against a railway, in 1828 the legislature
finally agreed to authorize it.

Meanwhile, the two regular canal sections were
begun. Surveyors moved in with their red stakes. Contractors built shanties and filled them with Irish laborers. And when the canal sections neared completion,
taverns, boarding houses, and shops were hammered
together. As in Ohio, prices of all supplies soared, making the canals more costly every day.

In four years, the shorter canal section at the western
end between Pittsburgh and Johnstown was entirely

completed. In two more years the middle canal section was ready for use. But people who wanted to go west by canal had to portage over the mountains in stagecoaches and wagons.

Meanwhile, other sections of the state that would not benefit from the Grand Canal were clamoring for branch canals. Their representatives stubbornly refused to appropriate more money for the main canal unless they could have their branch canals, too.

Much had already been spent on the Grand Canal. The most important and expensive section over the top of the Alleghenies had not yet been started. This main canal was expected to solve all the financial problems of the state; it could not be given up now. And so the legislature had to agree to appropriate money for the branch canals even though the state could not afford them.

As a result, contractors, laborers, and supplies were drawn off the Grand Canal. The work slowed down. It was not until 1834, eight years after it was authorized, that the entire stretch from Philadelphia to Pittsburgh was finished. By that time so much money had been spent that the state gave up the idea of continuing the channel to Lake Erie.

However, most citizens did not worry about the great debt. Here for 294 miles across the center of their state was one of the wonders of the world, far surpassing anything else that had been built in America. People would come from far away just to ride on it, and the tolls would take care of those petty problems that the legislature was worrying about.

Just as they had expected, everyone who could find the money took the four-day journey between Philadelphia and Pittsburgh. Most visitors to America included it on their list of marvelous things to do. Added to all these were the thousands of people who had been waiting to find homes for themselves in the West, even though they could go by canal only as far as Pittsburgh.

Day and night, the Grand Canal was crowded; boats loaded with travelers and freight were lined up at every lock and transfer point.

At first the railway west of Philadelphia provided only the rails. Anyone could use them. All he had to do was build a car with wheels that would fit onto the rails, hitch it to a horse or two, and put it onto the track wherever he liked. He could then go downhill toward Philadelphia or uphill toward Columbia, where the rails ended. There were no schedules or traffic rules.

Whenever eastbound and westbound cars met, the drivers fought for the right to stay on the track. Anyone else could join in the fight, and after some noses were bloodied and heads bashed, the victor pushed the other's car off the track and continued on his way.

This state of affairs could not last long. Soon the commissioners had to build double tracks. Before long the state took over the management and operation of the railroad. It provided the cars and a stationary engine at the top of the first rise to haul the cars up the steep incline—twenty-eight hundred feet long with a rise of 187 feet.

Much later it added some crude steam locomotives to pull the cars on west. Since these cars were open and the engines had to work up a great amount of steam, the passengers were often covered with smoke and showered with red-hot cinders. It was said that they were provided with buckets of sand for putting out fires in their clothing. But that was later.

In the 1830's, after that first stiff climb was maneuvered, fresh horses took over the hauling of the cars to a point near Columbia where another stationary engine let them down another hill. The trip lasted more than twenty hours. So far the passengers had not been on anything that could be called a canal or even a waterway.

But from Columbia a packet took the travelers on a real canal that meandered alongside the Susquehanna River. When it came to the junction of the Susquehanna and Juniata rivers, it entered a large pool of water created by a high dam.

For crossing the pool, the canal engineers had created something entirely new—a double-decked towpath bridge 2,231 feet long. One deck was for eastbound horses and drivers and the other was for westbound.

After the novel experience of being pulled across this pool by horses treading one of the strange towpaths, the passengers found themselves crossing the Juniata River on an aqueduct seven hundred feet long. Then the Grand Canal turned westward alongside the Juniata. In places where the engineers had been forced to dam the river, the boat actually entered the river for a short time.

At last the voyagers reached Hollidaysburg near the head of the Juniata River. They had traveled 172 miles by water and had gone through 108 locks. Now they faced the world-famous portage over the crest of the Allegheny mountain ridge by railroad.

They spent the night in Hollidaysburg. At 5:00 the next morning they were hustled out of bed and loaded into railroad cars. Horses drew them three and a half miles to the foot of the first inclined plane. There the horses were unhitched, the cars were attached to a strong cable, and the riders steeled themselves for the spectacular climb of more than a thousand feet.

Canvass White had devised an astonishing although complicated way of using the inclined plane theory to get the cars over the ridge. Ten inclined planes—five on each side of the mountain summit—were separated by level stretches of different lengths.

At the summit, two stationary steam engines drew one car up a plane while they let another car down a plane on the other side. On the level stretches between the inclined planes, where horses took over the job of pulling the cars, much hitching and unhitching consumed a great amount of time.

In some places the rails ran along the very edge of a precipice, causing much anxiety among the passengers who felt as though they were traveling through the air. Nevertheless, not one serious accident on the Portage Railway was ever recorded.

After this harrowing trip to the summit, the passengers were served a hearty breakfast at one of the two taverns. Then they boarded another car and went down the five inclined planes on the other side of the mountain.

At the bottom of the last inclined plane, one more thrill awaited them before they left the railway. A 901-foot tunnel, the longest in the whole country, carried them to the second canal.

At last they boarded another packet and rode on to Pittsburgh in comparative comfort even though they had to go through sixty-six locks in a little over a hundred miles.

Tourists did not seem to mind the slow progress through all these marvels of engineering. They were getting their money's worth. The Erie Canal was dull, indeed, compared with Pennsylvania's Grand Canal.

But for freight movers and westbound families the Pennsylvania Canal was slow and expensive. The cost of running the complicated mechanisms was so great that rates had to be increased until they were beyond the means of many families.

The Pennsylvania Canal never paid for itself, and the state was deeply in debt. Meanwhile, the Erie Canal, carrying emigrants westward in a continuous stream, was piling up such huge profits for New York that the legislators believed it would soon pay the expenses of the entire state.

10

Financial Disaster

One of the last states to be caught up in the canal craze was Indiana, but it was slow in getting under way. While other states were already digging their ditches, Indiana was still very thinly populated. Except in the river valleys the state was covered with dense hardwood forests, only occasionally broken by almost impassable wagon trails. The rivers were the only means of transportation for any distance.

The most important river to take people and produce across the state was the Wabash, 475 miles long. It rises just over the border in Ohio, runs west all the way across Indiana in the northern sector, and then cuts south along the western boundary until it empties into the Ohio River. It is a meandering waterway.

In those early days it was filled with rapids and

choked with rocks, fallen trees, and brush. But a sur-
prising number of people slowly made their way along
it, portaging their rafts and flatboats around the many
obstacles to reach the Ohio River or cut over to Illinois
on their way west.

Another river of importance at that time was the
Whitewater. It also empties into the Ohio River but on
the opposite side of Indiana. Because the earliest settlers had cleared land in the area, the river was a necessary although uncertain waterway for them.

The cry for internal improvements naturally had to
come to Indiana as it had come to other states. As early
as 1818, the governor asked the legislature to consider a
system of roads and canals. Soon a newspaper in Vin-
cennes, a village along the Wabash, was promoting its
own system of internal improvements.

But most of the backwoods settlers were so busy cutting down the huge trees, planting corn among the
stumps, and trying to live from one bout of the shakes
to another that they had little interest in big schemes
and certainly no money with which to pay for them.

Ever since George Washington had first pointed it
out, the federal government had been concerned that
only a six-mile portage through swamps separated two
important rivers in Indiana. These were the Wabash
and the Maumee, which were used for through traffic
to the West. About a year before the Erie Canal was
finished and before Ohio and Pennsylvania broke
ground for their canals, the Congress of the United
States donated to Indiana a corridor 320 feet wide

through public land for a short canal to replace the portage.

But this donation was not enough to satisfy the governor and the assembly. Three years later the federal government donated for the canal more than a third of a million acres, which the state accepted. The governor then set up a canal commission.

Still, there were delays because of constant bickering among different groups in the legislature. Some were Whitewater men, arguing for a canal to be built along the Whitewater River not only to give people a route into the unsettled interior of southeastern Indiana but also to provide themselves with a way to take their produce out.

Others called themselves Wabash men, advocating a much longer canal along the Wabash River to open the vast northern and western sections to settlement and prosperity. This canal would extend into Ohio and connect with the Miami and Erie Canal to draw immigrants to Indiana.

A good number of forward-looking men, including the governor, preferred railways. But these men were in the minority. The old argument that canals were more useful and more democratic because anyone could use them at any time was brought up again and again.

Not until 1831 was the decision made to proceed with the Wabash-Erie Canal. A commission was quickly appointed, an engineer was employed, and the surveying got under way.

Three times before, surveyors had waded into the

portage area to try to set red stakes. Two of the surveyors had died of malaria carried by the mosquitoes.
The third survived, but many of his helpers suc-
cumbed.

This time, however, the surveying was completed
and Washington's birthday, February 22, 1832, was
chosen for the ground-breaking ceremony at Fort
Wayne. Pennsylvania and Ohio were already learning
how costly and heartbreaking canals could be, but Indiana celebrated the great day with the usual wild excitement that lasted for weeks.

Backwoods settlers came from far away to take part.
Few of them were able to read or understand figures.
They simply believed what they were told. They would
soon have many neighbors and a fine way to market.
What more could they possibly want? Leave the worry
over money to the governor and the legislators whom
they had elected, they told themselves.

A fund commission was appointed and the many
acres of land donated by the federal government to pay
for the canal were put up for sale. But the results were
very disappointing. Only forty-two thousand acres
were sold for just seventy-five thousand dollars, one-
forth of it in cash. This was a mere fraction of what the
canal would surely cost.

Meanwhile, in the valleys of the Wabash and Maumee rivers near Fort Wayne, contractors put up shacks
and began to hire workmen. Since the state was so
sparsely settled, however, most of the workers had to
be brought in. In 1834, contractors had rounded up
about one thousand Irishmen. So many of these died

from swamp fevers or cholera that those who were still alive sometimes spent more hours digging graves than digging the canal. But more men were hired and the work went on.

As this first section neared completion, the board decided to extend the canal far across the state to Lafayette through a district inhabited almost entirely by Indians. Quickly and ruthlessly the Indians were pushed off the land and out of Indiana.

On July 4, 1835, a twenty-one-mile canal was opened with all the customary ceremony.

The excitement that followed the opening of this short stretch hit the state like an Indiana cyclone. Each area clamored for its own piece of internal improvement.

The internal improvements advocates controlled the legislature, each member insisting upon at least one special project for his own area. No legislator would vote for anyone else's project unless he was sure that his own would be voted in too.

So the members began a practice of trading votes, called logrolling. A certain number of legislators promised to vote for a Whitewater Canal if, in return, the Whitewater people would vote for a Central Canal. More votes were exchanged and projects were voted in until a huge Internal Improvements System was agreed upon and sent to the governor for his signature. It was mainly a list of major canals, but it also included railroads and turnpikes. Some smaller projects were marked for further study.

The whole system was estimated to cost thirteen million dollars—about one-sixth the wealth of the entire state. In all the excitement of exchanging votes, no one stopped to consider that Indiana could not possibly afford so many canals, railroads, and turnpikes. Few would believe that canals might ever become obsolete. Orators predicted that in a few years the improvements would not only pay for themselves but would also pay the cost of government and make taxation unnecessary.

Every town held its celebration with bonfires, illuminations, parades, and banquets. Meanwhile, land speculators went among the people buying and selling land along the routes for huge prices.

Nearly a year after that first small stretch of canal near Fort Wayne was opened, the governor appointed a six-man Board of Internal Improvements. This board instructed the old fund commission to float a loan for two million dollars. Bonds were handed out to the different members of the commission who advertised them for sale in different parts of the state and in the East.

Some of these commissioners had no idea how to handle such vast transactions. Some were plainly dishonest. They borrowed more than was authorized and then kept no records or receipts, or they took money for themselves and turned in false reports. But the mishandling of the money did not come to light for a while.

To make everyone happy, the Board of Internal Improvements decided to start all the projects at once. They handed out the work, like prizes, to the different members of a Board of Supervision.

Each member was given the work nearest his home. Suddenly he found that he was very popular. All his relatives, neighbors, friends, and even some former enemies wanted jobs—not as pick-and-shovel men but as supervisors, surveyors, and contractors. Whether they were qualified or not, they wanted the jobs that paid the highest salaries—and they got them.

The board members hired many unneeded special engineers, surveyors, and assistants at fantastic salaries for each project. When the rest of the people learned how many thousands of dollars these extra men cost the state, they angrily referred to them as the "Eating Brigade."

Starting all the projects at once destroyed the possibility of success for any of the projects. In the first place, there were not enough laborers to go around. Contractors bid against each other for workmen, and the wages went up. In a few years they were advertising in neighboring states that they would pay two dollars a day and guarantee roast beef for dinner. Compared with the usual six dollars a month, these were huge wages that added tremendously to the cost of construction.

Slowly, unconnected sections were finished. But until they could be connected, few tolls could be collected to begin to pay off the debt. On one project, completed by a thousand expensive laborers, the tolls for the first six months were only $670.

Some of the sections supervised by incompetent engineers did not perform as they were supposed to. Creeks or reservoirs, expected to furnish water, were dry. Or spring floods washed out the channels because no provision had been made to take care of overflow.

Surveyors spent $156,000 trying to decide whether to build a canal or a railway from Fort Wayne to Michigan City. But nothing at all came from this expenditure except great quantities of surveyors' notes.

Within a year after the Internal Improvements System had been passed, the legislators received a shocking financial report. Nearly four million dollars had been spent and the whole system would cost almost twice as much as had been estimated. They must now pay more than a million dollars every year for interest on the huge debt.

Taxes for the whole state brought in only forty-five thousand dollars that year.

When the governor was faced with the horrifying facts, he decided that the only way to get money for the interest was to borrow more money. But no one would lend any. This was the year 1837, when a financial depression was beginning to affect the whole country. Eastern banks were failing and money was scarce everywhere.

At last the governor announced that Indiana was bankrupt. It could not pay any more on its contracts.

Suddenly the wages of thousands of workers were cut off. Hundreds of contractors could not pay their bills totaling more than a million dollars. Eastern banks that had loaned money to the state demanded their interest. And Indiana's last hope, the federal government, refused to help.

An investigation of the financial affairs of the state was demanded.

The legislators attempted to straighten out the tangled accounts of the fund commission. But many of them were ignorant men who had been elected by their backwoods neighbors. They could not understand the money manipulations of dishonest men. Even the governor could not find out where the money had gone.

The only solution was to authorize banks to print more than a million dollars in treasury notes which the state could then borrow to pay off the contractors. Treasury notes were supposed to be redeemable in coins. But there was usually only a small amount of silver and gold in the banks and sometimes none at all.

When the people learned they had been swindled out of millions of dollars, they were furious. Members of the political parties, the Whigs and the Democrats, blamed each other. In time, however, they realized that blame would not solve their problems.

Beginning in 1840, the legislators tried to list the many projects in order of their importance. Some of the lawmakers wanted to complete them one at a time. Others wanted to cancel most of them.

A private company took over the Whitewater Canal, completed it, and finally connected it with Cincinnati, Ohio, in 1846. However, the valley through which the last section ran was too deep and narrow. In the next two years parts were destroyed by floods and had to be replaced.

Small sections in other parts of the state were either sold or abandoned. But many people felt that work on the important link between the East and the West, the Wabash and Erie Canal, must be completed. In 1842 the legislature ordered that it be continued southward to Terre Haute.

The bankrupt state decided to pay for work on the Wabash and Erie by issuing its own special kind of money, called scrip. Each time it printed a new batch of scrip it used a different color of paper—red or white or blue. People gave the phony money nicknames—Red Dog, White Dog, or Blue Dog. For a while, this was the only kind of money used along the canal.

At first it was accepted by merchants at full value. But when the canal finally reached a town and work crews moved on, the value of the scrip would drop to less than half and many merchants would go bankrupt.

Finally, in 1843, Ohio completed its part of the Wabash and Erie Canal and the two sections were joined. Boats that had been waiting across the state border entered Indiana in a continuous line bringing many thousands of settlers.

However, the banks that had loaned money to the state were pressing so hard for repayment that the legislature had to give up. It turned over the canal to its creditors. Even so, the state had a huge debt that must slowly be paid by the citizens through taxation. And the creditors were very unhappy, for some of them were almost bankrupt themselves and needed cash.

Although the Wabash and Erie Canal through Indiana did not always function well—sometimes flooding and sometimes going dry—it did give people along its channel a taste of life previously unknown to them.

Elaborate packets soon appeared. The fastest in the country, they caused a great stir among the settlers. They were painted in gaudy colors and were fitted out with expensive carpets, furniture, and china imported from Europe, the like of which few Indianians had ever seen.

Visitors from all over the world wanted to ride on the *Silver Bell*, painted silver inside and out and decorated with tinkling silver bells. It was drawn at eight miles an hour by silver gray mules with harness mountings of silver.

An Indiana packet had no schedule. It swept into the villages at any hour and gave the canalside people a great show. Since no beds or food were provided on board, the travelers in their fancy clothes strolled into the villages and knocked on doors for food and lodging. In the pioneer spirit, most of the settlers, glad for company and a little gossip, refused pay from their guests.

The canals also brought the poor settlers such prosperity as they had only dreamed of. Many became boat builders. Others quickly expanded their clearings and sold their produce for high prices. With their new wealth, they were able to buy necessities and even luxuries at a low price. The water power turned mills to grind their wheat into flour, so that they no longer had to walk many miles to have this work done. And with the building of docks, warehouses, stores, and hotels, their villages became towns that provided them with a welcome social life. They could ignore the fact that only a few miles back from the canal, the forests were as dense and unexplored as ever.

The state, excited by this new appearance of prosperity, decided to extend the Wabash and Erie all the way south to the Ohio River at Evansville, thus creating the longest canal in the country—457 miles. By this act, it was thought, Indiana would open more untouched territory for thousands of new settlers.

More scrip was printed, and workers were rounded up and sent into the area. Then troubles began. Oxen had to be used in the bottom lands to haul out the underbrush, for horses and mules were not strong enough to wade through the deep bogs. And the scrip depreciated so fast that contractors could not buy enough provisions. Laborers demanded their pay in hard cash, especially after diseases began to take a heavy toll. In one week, 150 men dropped dead while they were digging the channel.

During a hot August, portions of the canal went dry. Villagers warred with each other over the scant amount of water that remained. Two neighboring towns went so far as to block each other's water supply, defending their rights with loaded rifles. But they gained nothing.

The extension southward from Terre Haute was a failure. Floods broke the banks and aqueducts. When an order came to close any part of the Wabash and Erie Canal that was not paying expenses, all the part below

Terre Haute was closed at once. The rest of the canal operated off and on for a few more years.

Of all the canals built in America in the nineteenth century, the Wabash and Erie seemed to have been the greatest failure. Yet, when it was operating, it moved many thousands of people into the state and on to Illinois and beyond. If the state had concentrated upon building only the one canal, it might have been a great success.

11

End of an Era

In the ten years after the Erie Canal was opened, while the crush of migrating people doubled and redoubled, prices of land along the Erie grew so high that a poor New England farmer could not buy even a foot of it. Before line boats drew up at the Utica wharf, everyone on board had heard that eleven canalside lots had been sold for a million dollars.

From east-going boats came the news that an acre of land in Toledo, Ohio, bought from the government for $1.25, had been sold for $100 for each foot fronting a canal that was not yet completed. And the word from the Atlantic shore was that fifty thousand foreigners were reaching America every year to fan out over the new land.

Travelers began to panic. Where could they go? Not to Ohio any more, they thought, with land selling at such prices. Not to Indiana, where canal debts were going to be loaded upon the people for generations.

Some suggested Michigan and the idea spread. As yet there were no canals in Michigan Territory. Land was still cheap. Families could get there by Great Lakes steamships.

The movement toward Michigan took hold, even though few could point out the territory on a map. A song reverberated from one Erie line boat to another, with *Michigan* changed to *Michigania* to rhyme with *way* and *stay*, two important words in the vocabulary of the land seekers:

Come all ye Yankee farmers who wished to change
*   your lot,*
Who've spunk enough to travel beyond your native
*   spot,*
And leave behind the village where Pa and Ma do stay,
Come follow me, and settle in Michigania,—
Yea, yea, yea, in Michigania.

Then there's the State of New York where some are
*   very rich;*
Themselves and a few others have dug a mighty ditch,
To render it more easy for us to find the way
And sail upon the waters to Michigania,—
Yea, yea, yea, to Michigania.

Soon an average of three steamboats reached Detroit every day, carrying from two to three hundred passengers. A large one, the *United States*, brought seven hundred. They crowded into land offices to buy government land which they had no time to inspect beforehand.

With so many newcomers in the territory, the governing fathers decided that their state too must have internal improvements. In 1836 they floated five million dollars of bonds for many canals, railroads, and turnpikes. The bonds were quickly taken up by brokers. Soon, however, the financial panic bankrupted everyone, and Michigan lost its money.

Although the territory was left with a five million dollar debt, its people were lucky. No canals were built; no additional crushing debts for construction, maintenance, and graft were imposed upon them.

Not so in Illinois. The possibility of a canal in the territory that later became the state of Illinois had been first suggested in 1673 by the French explorer Louis Joliet. In fact, this first suggestion for a canal in all of America was destined to be the last in the canal-craze era.

Sharing great hardships with Father Jacques Marquette, Joliet had arrived at Lake Michigan where the city of Chicago now stands. Between Chicago and what was later named the Illinois River, he found a short, marshy stretch of land. When strong winds came from the east, water from Lake Michigan blew through this marsh and flowed on down the Illinois River. A canal here, he said, would open an easy route from Lake Michigan all the way to New Orleans and onward to the French territory of Florida.

The idea that Louis Joliet had first expressed was excellent, but no one did anything significant about it for nearly 150 years. The War Department, making a survey in 1819, noted this possible passage. Three years later a southern Illinois newspaper argued for it. The legislature of 1822–23 passed a canal bill, set up a commission, and ordered that a survey and estimate of cost be made. Still, there was little money for such a project.

Although a good number of people lived in Illinois, most of them had settled in the southern part of the state. Quite early, groups of French emigrants had traveled up the Mississippi to the prairie land. Later, Easterners had made the grueling trek over the mountains and down the Ohio River to southern Illinois. These people could see no need for a waterway to the little northern village of Chicago which, in 1825, had only fourteen taxpayers.

In 1827, Congress gave public land for internal improvements to Illinois. After many arguments, the state senate ordered a report on the possibility of a railroad or turnpike over the same route. But nothing was accomplished by this order, either, except on paper.

At last, in 1834, a forceful Illinois statesman named Joseph Duncan was elected governor. He favored canals over railroads. Although he had to work with a legislature that was sharply divided between canals and railroads and between northern and southern attitudes, he was finally able to see a bill passed that provided for the Illinois and Michigan Canal.

But the arguing did not stop. Here, as in Indiana,

people from different parts of the state wanted something for themselves. The legislature of 1835–36 granted more than a dozen charters for railroads. These did not follow any large-scale or useful plan. They were merely short sections here and there in the state to satisfy the different factions.

The following year it added to the confusion by passing "An Act to establish and maintain a General System of Internal Improvements." It appropriated ten million dollars that it did not have—all for roads and railroads.

Meanwhile, because of the canal that was to be built, Chicago became a booming town. Steamers arrived daily, bringing thousands of eager land buyers. Boardinghouses and hotels were pounded together; still there was not room enough for all the new people.

The mud of the stump-dotted streets was so spongy that people could sink to their waists if they tried to get from one side to the other. But in this carnival atmosphere, no one seemed to care. Deeds and down payments changed hands here many times each day.

Land speculators went wild. They put fantastic prices on land within miles of the proposed canal route. They plotted mythical towns on paper, gave them fancy names, and sold lots in them to eastern and even European investors. "Paper towns," they were called, for they existed only on a piece of paper in a fast talker's pocket.

On a hot July 4, 1836, boatloads of important people moved up the Chicago River to Bridgeport while the

ordinary people walked along Archer Road. Everyone
was in a mood to celebrate, including all the Irish who
had been brought in to do the digging of the canal.

After the speeches, the first spadeful of dirt was
lifted for a canal that was planned to be big enough for
steamboats. Freight, it was said, would go directly by
steamboat from Chicago to the Illinois River and on
down the Mississippi without being reloaded. Or
steamers could go from Chicago through the Great
Lakes to Buffalo, reloading only once for the Erie
Canal run to New York City. Chicago would become
the great grain center of America.

Stakes were set and a little dirt was taken out before
the financial crash of 1836 hit Illinois with special
ferocity and stopped the work for a number of years.

Although a crash was bound to follow the fantastic
rise in land prices, it was hastened by President An-
drew Jackson, who suddenly decreed that all government land must be paid for in gold or silver instead of
the sometimes worthless paper money. People rushed
to the banks to take out hard money, and the banks
closed their doors. Even so, there was only a little silver
and gold in the state, certainly not enough to make the
huge payments on land purchases.

By 1837, depression spread over the entire country.
People in Illinois had lost not only the land but their
down payments. The value of the land went back to its
original $1.25 per acre, and those who had been carried
away by the craze were bankrupt.

The Illinois Board of Public Works tried to continue

all the different projects that had been authorized. But here, as in Indiana, graft took the bulk of the money. By 1839, the people were aware of what was happening. As a Peoria newspaper said, the engineering department was "rotten from the core to the surface."

In the East, the crash was felt just as keenly. Everything came to a standstill. All building ended, leaving partly finished homes, stores, and factories. Nine out of ten factories closed. Hundreds of banks shut their doors for good.

People without land or any way of raising food for their families were starving. They rioted in the city streets, broke open warehouses, and carried away food.

The depression that spread through every part of the land lasted for more than four years. But the movement westward continued as before. Anyone who had saved enough money to take his family on a line boat or hammer together some sort of craft left the stricken East in search of a piece of cheap land.

On the other hand, the enthusiasm for building and maintaining canals that would place greater tax burdens upon bankrupt states quickly died out. The depression that continued past 1840 was the beginning of the end of the canal era, although few realized it at the time.

A private company, with financial help from Ohio, was caught in the midst of building the Pennsylvania and Ohio Canal from Cleveland to Pittsburgh. It struggled through to completion in 1840, thus opening what was considered one of the most important canals in the country. It provided another way from the East to Lake Erie, a route that was shorter than the Erie Canal and free of ice for a few weeks longer.

Commissioner Kelley borrowed money personally to finish the Miami and Erie Canal to Lake Erie and also the extension to meet the Wabash and Erie at the Indiana border, but the work dragged on. The two canals were finally finished in 1843, after the depression had lifted and Ohio bonds were acceptable again.

Pennsylvania's Grand Canal always spent more than it took in. The depression foreshadowed the end for this great engineering feat.

Indiana could not even try to pay its debts.

In 1835, a plan for widening and deepening the Erie Canal had been undertaken. This canal, always a financial success, continued to thrive throughout the depression. When it was apparent that packets were only a nuisance and no longer made money for the state, they were taken off the canal. But the waterway was a very important freight line for many years.

However, the branch canals that had been authorized became too expensive during this period of financial trouble. In 1842, a "stop law" halted all canal work in the state of New York.

During the years of depression, the few railroads that had been started shared the same fate as the canals. When work stopped, road beds crumbled. Weeds and underbrush choked the cuts.

Early railroads had been much less satisfactory than canals. Horses pulled the cars on wooden rails that quickly rotted. The tracks were often washed out by heavy rains or floods.

Gradually, however, iron caps were put on the wooden rails, and primitive steam engines replaced the horses. But they had to stop every six miles to take on wood and water, and often the passengers were required to help.

While all the work on internal improvements was at a standstill, violent arguments were carried on everywhere on the advantages of canals versus possible future railways.

Those who favored canals usually brought up the same old idea that canals were more democratic. Then there was the indisputable argument that the materials for canals—stone, wood, and clay—could be found anywhere in America while the new steam engines and iron rails had to be imported from England, so recently America's enemy.

Other arguments against railroads were plentiful. The engines were hazardous. They showered sparks that set off forest or prairie fires and endangered the people who rode the trains. And the engines had a tendency to blow up. The body, it was believed, could not withstand a speed of twenty miles an hour behind one of those iron monsters. The blood would boil, and the passengers would collapse.

Farmers feared the terrifying effects of the noisy black beasts dashing through their farmlands. Cows would be so frightened that they would not give milk. Chickens would not lay eggs.

On the other side of the debate was the deep-seated resentment over the terrible debts for canals and the taxes that had to be paid.

Although many people tried to defend the canals, others could find nothing good to say about them. Gradually resentment turned to hatred for the very waterways that once had seemed so desirable. Canals were accused of causing every sickness, from the shakes to boils. They were hated for draining off water from creeks and streams.

Gangs of men broke locks, cut aqueducts, tore down towpaths and berms, and dumped rocks into the channels.

They were aided by the inability of the states to keep the canals in repair. When floods overflowed channels and tore holes in towpaths, when locks sprang leaks, only futile attempts were made to halt the damage. In time, farmers scraped the dirt of the towpaths and berms into abandoned sections of the ditches and planted crops over them.

Meanwhile, railroad engineers had been making improvements on those first unsatisfactory engines. They planned roadbeds that would be raised several feet above the surrounding land. These would be built of crushed rock that would drain easily.

As soon as the depression began to lift, railroad companies were formed by Eastern capitalists. Soon they began to construct their lines all over the country.

Many thousands of out-of-work laborers were brought into Illinois to build the roadbed for 765 miles of track. They were poorly paid, ragged, and subject to every sickness that came along. But in 1856 they finished laying the tracks for the Illinois Central Railway, much of the line through uninhabited prairies.

The Pennsylvania Railroad Company began a roadbed alongside the state's Grand Canal. In 1857, it bought the bankrupt canal system for only $7,500,000.

Since parts of the canal system had actually been railroads, the new owners used many miles of the old roadbed for their own line after ripping up the worn rails and sending them to Indiana for a railroad across the northern part of that state. On some short sections of the canal waterway they hauled coal in barges to supply the locomotives with fuel.

Quickly the new companies invaded the other states that had so proudly built canals. Soon they ran their lines alongside canals that were still operating. They cut their rates in summer when the canals were hauling freight, thus ruining the canal business. In winter, when they had no competition, they raised their rates. Sometimes they even ran their tracks across the waterways.

Only two of the important canals—the first and the last—were able to hold out against the competition of the railroads. The Erie Canal was widened and deepened from time to time. Double locks, like those at Lockport, were built to keep the traffic moving.

It was a financial success all through the Civil War and beyond. In fact, in the early 1870's, it carried more freight than ever before. In 1882, it had brought so much wealth to the state that all tolls could be abolished.

The mighty Erie Canal slowed down the development of railroads in the state of New York. But in time it too had to give way. Most of it was filled in. Where it cut through cities, it was paved over.

Later, a great barge canal was dug across the state to continue the work of the Erie, but in a much larger way.

The Illinois and Michigan Canal was finally completed from Chicago to La Salle on the Illinois River in 1848. Because the route was relatively level, the canal was not difficult to build.

Even though it was completed at a time when railroads were very popular, it was a great financial success during its short life. The freight that it carried made Chicago rich beyond all the dreams of its builders. This last canal of the era, and one of the smallest, in its own way accomplished for Chicago what the great Erie Canal had accomplished for New York City.

But in 1871 Chicago decided to use the canal to carry off excess sewage. It seemed destined to die, like most of the other canals.

Years later, however, the federal government took it over and constructed a nine-foot channel which it completed in 1933 as an important link in the Lakes to Gulf Waterway.

Except for a few carefully preserved relics, in only occasional places can one now see any remnants of the canals built during the first part of the nineteenth cen-

tury. A broken-down lock, moss-covered and deserted
—a crumbling foundation for an aqueduct—a depression across a farmer's field, once a part of a channel—
these are all that remain of the several thousand miles
of canals that carried hundreds of thousands of people
westward.

Yet these same canals, so quickly forgotten, had
changed the whole character of our country within the
short span of twenty to thirty years.

At the beginning of the canal era, all economic and
social development was concentrated along a strip of
land in the East. Piling up behind the mountain barrier
was an ever-increasing population impatiently waiting
for the dam to break.

As soon as the first breakthrough came, the canals set
off the greatest migration in the history of America.
They also triggered a mass emigration from other countries to the new land.

The canals were the great levelers, mixing different
classes and nationalities into that huge body of people
called Americans, while they moved them ever westward.

For Further Reading

Adams, Samuel Hopkins. *The Erie Canal*. New York: Random House, 1953.

Andrist, Ralph K. *The Erie Canal*. New York: American Heritage Publishing Co., Inc., 1964.

Buley, R. Carlyle. *The Old Northwest Pioneer Period, 1815–1840*, 2 vols. Indianapolis, Indiana: Indiana Historical Society, 1950.

Franchere, Ruth. *The Travels of Colin O'Dae*. New York: Thomas Y. Crowell Company, 1966.

Greenleaf, Barbara Kaye. *American Fever: The Story of American Immigration*. New York: Four Winds Press, 1970.

Harlow, Alvin F. *Old Towpaths*. New York: D. Appleton and Company, 1926. Reprinted by Kennikat Press, Inc., 1964.

Payne, Robert. *The Canal Builders*. Chapter 6. New York: The Macmillan Company, 1959.

Waggoner, Madeline Sadler. *The Long Haul West.* New York: G. P. Putnam's Sons, 1958.

Wilcox, Frank. *The Ohio Canals*. Kent, Ohio: Kent State University Press, 1969.

Wyld, Lionel D. *Low Bridge! Folklore and the Erie Canal*. Syracuse, New York: Syracuse University Press, 1962.

Index